Cambridge Latin Course

Book I
Teacher's Guide

FOURTH EDITION

CAMBRIDGE
UNIVERSITY PRESS

CAMBRIDGE UNIVERSITY PRESS
Cambridge, New York, Melbourne, Madrid, Cape Town, Singapore, São Paulo, Delhi

Cambridge University Press
The Edinburgh Building, Cambridge CB2 8RU, UK

www.cambridge.org
Information on this title: www.cambridge.org/9780521648592

This book, an outcome of work jointly commissioned by the Schools Council
before its closure and the Cambridge School Classics Project, is published under
the aegis of Qualifications and Curriculum Authority Enterprises Limited,
29 Bolton Street, London W1Y 7PD.

First published 1970
Second edition 1982
This edition 1999
8th printing 2008

Printed in the United Kingdom at the University Press, Cambridge

A catalogue record for this publication is available from the British Library

ISBN 978-0-521-64859-2 paperback

Layout by Newton Harris Design Partnership
Illustrations by Kathy Baxendale

CONTENTS

Cambridge Latin Course Book I

Stage	Name	Cultural background	Main language features
1	**Caecilius**	Pompeii: Caecilius' household; houses in Pompeii.	Word order in sentences with **est**. Word order in sentences without **est**. Nominative singular.
2	**in vīllā**	Pompeii: daily life and food.	Nominative and accusative singular. Sentence pattern NOMINATIVE + ACCUSATIVE + VERB.
3	**negōtium**	Pompeii: town life and business.	Nominative and accusative of 1st, 2nd and 3rd declensions.
4	**in forō**	The forum at Pompeii; finance and the law courts.	1st and 2nd person singular present, including **sum**, **es**.
5	**in theātrō**	The theatre: actors and performances; pantomime, comedy.	Nominative plural. 3rd person plural present.
6	**Fēlīx**	Slaves and freedmen.	Imperfect and perfect (**v**-stems) in 3rd person singular and plural. **erat** and **erant**.
7	**cēna**	Roman beliefs about life after death.	Sentence pattern ACCUSATIVE + VERB. Perfect tense (other than forms in **v**).
8	**gladiātōrēs**	The amphitheatre and gladiatorial shows.	Accusative plural. Superlative.
9	**thermae**	The Roman baths.	Dative singular and plural.
10	**rhētor**	The Roman education system; books and writing.	1st and 2nd person plural present including **esse**. Comparative.
11	**candidātī**	Pompeii: elections and local government.	Intransitive verbs with dative. Sentence pattern NOMINATIVE + DATIVE + VERB. **placet**. **nōbīs** and **vōbīs**. Different ways of asking questions.
12	**Vesuvius**	The eruption of Vesuvius; the destruction and excavation of Pompeii.	1st and 2nd person (singular and plural) imperfect and perfect. 1st and 2nd person (singular and plural) imperfect of **esse**.

PREFACE

It is more than 25 years since the *Cambridge Latin Course* was first published. It is now established as the most popular Latin course used in schools, with the specially designed School Classics Project GCSE examinations offered by OCR and AQA attracting more than half of the total Latin entries in 1998. The Course is also used in a number of countries overseas, particularly in North America where there is a separate edition to meet the needs of the American and Canadian market. There is also a separate North American Cambridge Classics Project, which came into existence thanks to the enthusiasm and commitment of Professor Ed Phinney from the University of Massachusetts, who sadly died in 1996.

The Course last underwent a major revision at the beginning of the 1980s, when the shortcomings of the first edition were addressed very successfully by Robin Griffin using evidence from an extensive evaluation exercise. Since then the Project has produced independent learning materials and worksheet master exercises to supplement the Course, and introduced a graded test scheme to provide students with a record of their progress during the Course.

The integrated edition has stood the test of time well, and no attempt has been made in this revision to make any substantial changes to the linguistic structure or the main story line of the Course. Nevertheless, there have been pressing reasons for revising the Course again, namely:

- the need for a more attractive format;
- the steady reduction in time allocated to Latin up to GCSE.

While the Project has been keen to bring out a colour edition for a long time, this has only become possible with the emergence of new technologies making colour printing more affordable. The new edition of Book I contains more than 150 colour photographs which will enrich the students' learning experience and enable them, more than ever before, to place the language they are learning in the cultural context of Pompeii in the first century AD.

The reduction in time for teaching Latin has been a more difficult issue to address. Given that the Course is based on the principle that students should learn the Latin through reading, any substantial reduction in reading material is likely to undermine the learning process. Nevertheless, a few stories have been removed where their omission has not affected the story line, and others have been shortened. Comprehension questions have been tightened up and revised, and their number has been increased, with marks allocated for each question and a mark scheme provided in this Guide.

The Guide is the result of a thorough revision of the earlier Handbook and the new format provides greater clarity and ease of use. The Guide includes notes on all the illustrations. We are indebted to Jill Dalladay for tackling the Handbook revision with such efficiency and flair.

We should also like to thank Fiona Kelly, Commissioning Editor at Cambridge University Press, for her encouragement and patience, as well as technical expertise, throughout the revision process.

We have been very fortunate in being able to enlist a talented revision team and we should like to express our thanks to the following: the members of the Working Party, Eileen Emmett, Jean Hubbard and Pam Perkins, who contributed so many ideas and materials; Maire Collins, the Project Secretary, who produced countless drafts with her customary precision and good humour; Patricia Acres, Roger Davies, Robin Griffin, Debbie James, John Patterson, Meg Thorpe, Margaret Widdess and Julie Wilkinson.

Finally, we wish to record our gratitude to all the teachers who continue to support the Project and whose constructive comments at conferences and in correspondence have informed the thinking of the revision team.

Bob Lister, Director
Pat Story, Revision Editor
Roger Dalladay, Picture Editor

INTRODUCTION

The case for Latin

There are strong reasons for teaching Latin, particularly as a reading course.

Interest. Latin is intrinsically interesting to anyone who likes people, ideas, words, the past or studying the way society works.

Understanding of language. The study of Latin provides students with an insight into the structure of an inflected language and encourages them to make instructive comparisons with their own language. They learn that many English words are derived from Latin and improve their command of their own language by adding to their vocabulary. They develop a sound basis for the study of Romance languages such as French, Spanish and Italian, and an understanding of how they are related through their origins in Latin.

Literary appreciation. To develop critical insight into the way language is used to express feelings, to develop trains of thought or to influence people, is a central aim of education.

Historical understanding. The period of the Roman Empire is a key epoch of European history; it offers an excellent opportunity to learn about the past through primary sources in the form of written evidence and archaeological remains.

Our origins. Through Latin, students gain insight into elements of western European and other societies: language, literature, law, attitudes to religion, civil engineering and technology, and political structures.

Careers. For degree studies in some subjects – e.g. English, law, history, modern languages – a basic understanding of Latin is still a considerable advantage.

The National Curriculum and the Cambridge Latin Course. The Course contributes to the National Curriculum in all the ways described above. It improves literacy and promotes literary appreciation. Based on authentic material about the Roman Empire, it helps develop skills in handling historical evidence. It can provide material for modules on ethical and moral issues in Religious Education or citizenship courses, for imaginative and argumentative essays or oral presentations for GCSE English, or for samples of work for Information and Communication Technology (ICT) portfolios.

The *Cambridge Latin Course*

Aims and principles

1 The Course has two main aims. The first is to teach comprehension of the Latin language for reading purposes. The second is to develop from the

outset an understanding of the content, style and values of Roman civilisation, with special reference to the 1st century AD. The Course presents language not as an end in itself, but as a means of gaining access to literature and to the culture from which it springs.

2 The Course seeks to present students with material that will arouse and maintain their interest. Motivated students are more likely to make the effort to master the language and gain more knowledge and understanding of Roman culture and literature.

3 Language and culture are integrated from the very outset by using as much authentic Roman subject matter as possible. The Course is set firmly in a Roman context and frequently introduces historical characters. Its systematic presentation of social, political and historical aspects of Roman culture is both a valuable part of general education and an essential preparation for the reading of Roman authors.

4 Information about Roman culture is conveyed not only in the text of the Latin stories and the section in English in each Stage, but also by the many illustrations. These provide the student with visual evidence of the Roman world and are meant to be studied and discussed in conjunction with the text.

5 The Course draws a distinction between *knowledge about* the language and *skill in using* the language. Many students who appear to understand linguistic information presented in isolation find it hard to apply that information in their reading. In the Course, reading experience precedes discussion and analysis. Comments on the language are elicited from students rather than presented to them.

6 Students are introduced from the beginning to common phrase and sentence patterns of the language which are systematically developed throughout the Course. Inflections and constructions are presented within these patterns in a controlled and gradual sequence. It is important that students should understand the form and function of the words that make up a sentence or phrase, and equally important that they should develop the habit of grouping words together and treating the phrase or sentence as a single unit. Language learning consists of forming habits as well as solving problems.

7 The development of reading skill requires appropriate teaching methods:
   (a) Comprehension questions are widely used to assist and test understanding and pave the way for the later approach to literature.
   (b) Translation is a most useful learning and testing device, but is not all important and sometimes can be dispensed with. The criterion for its use should be the degree to which it contributes to an intelligent understanding of what is read.
   (c) Vocabulary is best acquired through attentive reading and oral

work in class, reinforced by revision of selected common words in checklists.

(d) Memorisation of the paradigm of a verb or noun should not be undertaken in isolation. It cannot contribute to the reading skill unless students also learn to recognise the function of inflections in the context of a Latin text.

Composition exercises from English into Latin do not contribute sufficiently to the development of reading skill to justify their inclusion in a reading course.

Course certification

Graded tests approved by the Secretary of State for Education and Employment are available from the Cambridge School Classics Project, to assess progress at intervals during the Course. Successful students receive a certificate which can be recorded in their National Record of Achievement. The tests provide a satisfying conclusion for those who do not continue their studies as far as GCSE.

Two GCSE examinations are provided for students who have followed the Course. Syllabuses may be obtained from Oxford Cambridge and RSA (OCR) and Assessment Qualifications Alliance (AQA).

The content of the Course

The students' material consists of Books I–V, divided into Stages. Book I, set in Pompeii in the 1st century AD, is based on the **familia** of Lucius Caecilius Iucundus, whose house and business records survive; Book II introduces two very different parts of the Roman Empire, Britain and Egypt; Book III returns to Britain, in particular to Bath and the fortress at Chester; Books IV and V are set in the city of Rome and focus on life and politics in the imperial court.

Each Stage contains new language features and deals with a different aspect of Roman culture; there is, in most cases, a standard format.

Model sentences. New language features are presented in a coherent context of whole sentences or short paragraphs, accompanied by line drawings.

Latin stories. Narrative and dramatic passages form the core of each Stage. They have a developing story line, and a context related to the aspect of Roman culture featured in the Stage. They are the main means of consolidating the language, and increase in length and complexity as the Course advances. New vocabulary is given alongside, in the form in which it appears in the text.

About the language. An explanation is provided of language features that have been introduced or have occurred frequently in the Stage. It usually appears some way into the Stage and is designed to be studied after students have become familar with the language features through the stories.

Practising the language. Exercises consolidate important features of language which have been introduced in the current Stage or encountered previously.

Cultural background material. This provides an explanation of the aspect of Roman culture featured in the Stage and forms the context or subject matter of the Latin stories. It may contain extracts from Roman writers or archaeological findings and is copiously illustrated.

Vocabulary checklist. At the end of each Stage there is a list of common words which have occurred several times in the text and should now be known. In the early Stages, nouns and adjectives are presented in the nominative singular, and verbs in the 3rd person singular. The Course gradually brings in the traditional key grammatical forms until finally the principal parts of verbs, the three genders of adjectives, and the genitive and gender of nouns are listed. Students are thus equipped to use a Latin dictionary.

Language information. This section at the end of each Book summarises the language content of the Book; in Books II–V it also builds on the language features encountered in previous Books. It contains grammatical tables, notes, additional exercises and a general vocabulary.

Supplementary materials

Available from Cambridge University Press:

- *Worksheet Masters*. Additional exercises for Books I and II. For each Stage there is an exercise on the stories, language features, derivations and the cultural background, and an aural and a visual exercise. The sheets are designed for students to write on, and may be photocopied.
- Audio recordings of dramatised readings from Books I–V.

Available from the Cambridge School Classics Project:

- *Graded Tests Booklets*. To use for summative assessment at intervals during the Course.
- *Independent Learning Manuals*. For Books I and II. Designed for students with limited time in class. Many teachers have found these a useful source of material and ideas, especially when classes encompass a wide range of ability. Each Stage ends with a short language test.
- *Independent Learning Answer Books*.

Course planning

You need to build balance, variety and progression into the course in order to help students achieve the success of which they are capable.

1 Plan the whole course in advance, identifying targets and drawing up a timetable. In some schools a 1 year Foundation Course is planned for all students, with a smaller group continuing the course to GCSE. It is possible to plan a coherent course based on Book I, or on Books I and II, culminating in a graded test.

For those teaching a GCSE examination group, the following outlines are suggested for 3 and 4 year courses. As time allowances vary widely, modifications may have to be made.

Four year course	*Three year course*
Year 1: Book I, Book II (Roman Britain)	Year 1: Book I, Book II
Year 2: Book II (Alexandria), Book III	Year 2: Book III, Book IV and start
Year 3: Book IV, Book V (part)	GCSE set texts
Year 4: Book V (remainder), GCSE set texts	Year 3: Book V and GCSE set texts.

A 2 year GCSE course should be attempted only with able students and a generous weekly time allowance.

2 Whatever the length of your course, you should regularly include elements of: story line, linguistic material, cultural and historical context, teacher-aided reading with discussion to develop literary response, and independent reading of the easier stories.

3 Set students an exercise in translation or comprehension on a regular basis as homework or classwork. The advantage of classwork is that you can monitor students' progress directly and give help as needed. Use the stories in the Course for those exercises so that the story line (and therefore the students' motivation) is sustained.

4 Build in both formative and summative assessment.

5 Some stories will have to be omitted by those moving quickly through the Course, e.g.:

Stage 3 **in forō** (p. 28)	Stage 8 **pāstor et leō** (p. 104)
Stage 4 Exercise 2, **Grumiō et leō** (p. 47)	Stage 9 **in apodytēriō** (p. 122)
Stage 5 Exercise 3, **in theātrō** (p. 63)	Stage 10 **statuae** (p. 137)
Stage 6 Exercise 1, **avārus** (pp. 76–7)	Stage 11 **Lūcius Spurius Pompōniānus**
Stage 7 **post cēnam** (p. 89)	(pp. 151–3).

You will need to fill in the gaps for the class, in both language and story line. For example, translate the whole story to the class, keeping them involved by giving them the occasional word or phrase to translate or by asking comprehension questions.

6 Stick to your timetable, making further cuts if necessary, so that you do not have a crisis at the end. In preparing for GCSE, allow adequate time for appreciative study of the set books. They are more difficult for students because they lack the built-in support of the course material. Be prepared to duplicate helpful notes and set examination-type questions for practice.

7   Give students their own copy of the overall timetable for the course so
    that they can be partners in keeping up the pace, and gain motivation
    from noting their progress. They should also be given a more detailed
    breakdown for each term.

Teaching method

The suggestions below are based on the principles of the Course, and offer
a starting-point from which you can develop strategies of your own
according to the needs of your students.

Model sentences. A possible sequence for handling these is:
1   Set the scene so that students begin to understand the cultural context
    of the new Stage. This can be done by:
    (a) Brief discussion of the picture on the opening page.
    (b) Quick reference to the line drawings.
    (c) Introducing the background material during a previous lesson or
        setting it as homework.
2   Read aloud a group of sentences in Latin, slowly enough to be clear and
    distinct, and give students time to understand them.
3   Ask questions, in English, carefully designed to elicit correct, concrete
    answers, e.g.: **spectātōrēs in theātrō sedent** (p. 56)

Who are in the picture?	Spectators.
Are they standing, walking or sitting?	Sitting.
Where?	In the theatre.
So what does the whole sentence mean?	The spectators are sitting in the theatre.

4   Pass quickly on to the next sentence or group of sentences. Allow
    students to discover the sense of the new feature for themselves,
    without explanation from you. The context provides clear clues, and
    experience shows that students often arrive at the right meaning after
    the first or second example.
5   If a sentence has proved confusing, repeat it before moving on.
    Otherwise, sustain momentum by a quick pace of question and answer,
    and a swift transition from one sentence to the next.
6   A second run-through of all the sentences is advisable, perhaps at the
    beginning of the next lesson.

Latin stories. These form a large part of each Stage and variety of
approach is essential.
1   *Planning*
    (a) Divide a story into sections to be handled one at a time. Make sure
        that each section makes sense in itself. Occasionally the class may be
        divided into groups, each of which (given a rough idea of the story
        line) prepares a different section of the story for the rest.

(b) Different parts of a story may present varying levels of difficulty, and need varying treatment, e.g.:

Easy paragraphs. Read aloud in Latin, ask students to study the paragraph in pairs or groups, and check their understanding by asking comprehension questions; or ask students to explore individually, and then translate orally.

Difficult paragraphs. Read aloud in smaller sections. Ask the whole group to suggest the meaning of individual words or phrases, gradually building up collectively the meaning of sentences and eventually the paragraph. Alternatively, read aloud with pauses to ask more knowledgeable students the meaning of key words or phrases. Groups then explore the passage. Use comprehension questions to advance the group's understanding, follow up with translation.

(c) Similarly, when reading easy stories, students can work independently, whereas more guidance will be needed with difficult stories.

2   *Introducing a story.* Strategies include the following.

Looking back. Reviewing a previous story, possibly anticipating how particular characters may react, or highlighting elements of the plot that are left unresolved.

Visual stimulus. Discussing illustrations or showing slides to present the visual setting.

Aural stimulus. Reading the story aloud in a lively and dramatic manner (or playing a taped reading) while students follow the text, gleaning some hints of the plot.

Looking forward. Raising questions to which students will discover answers.

3   *The first reading.* Here the aim is to establish the general sense.

(a) Read the first section of the story aloud in Latin with students following the text. There is a guide to the pronunciation of Latin in the *Independent Learning Manuals* and *Graded Tests Booklets*. It is essential that students are introduced to a passage by hearing it read aloud well. When they hear the words organised into phrases or clauses, and the characters differentiated, they glean clues to the meaning. They should regularly read the Latin aloud themselves, observing phrase and clause boundaries.

(b) Give students time to study the text for themselves, using the vocabulary and any other help available. It is important to provide a supportive context that maximises their chances of success. Sometimes organise them in groups or pairs so that they can help each other. The teacher should circulate, giving encouragement and help, and noting on the board or OHP any points that will later need clarification.

With straightforward passages, students may be briefed from the outset to produce:

- A summary of the main points (written or oral).
- An oral or written translation.
- A chart, map or drawing for a topographical passage.
- A mime or a play of the incident described.

(c) Check students' understanding by asking for feedback from the groups or conducting a question-and-answer session. For example, questions on the first paragraph of **Fēlīx** (Stage 6, p. 72) might include:
What were the Pompeians doing?
What were they drinking? Where?
Were there many or few Pompeians in the inn?
What did Clemens do?
Whom did Clemens see? How did he greet him?
Fēlīx erat lībertus. What does **lībertus** mean? Who do you think freed him?

(d) Diagnose the source of any difficulties by taking the class slowly through problem sentences. Distinguish between uncertainty caused by forgetting the meaning of words and failure to understand a relatively new language feature, e.g. omission of subject, apposition or subordinate clause.

(e) Work on any difficulties. The purpose of the first reading is to understand the meaning of the Latin, not to analyse the language. Two techniques are especially useful:

- Rephrasing or expanding questions to enable students to understand the Latin for themselves, e.g. (for the first paragraph of **Fēlīx**): 'Who were the people in the inn? Who came into the inn?'
- Taking the students back to a familiar sentence with the same structure. Students often remember the model sentences and will quickly see the similarity.

(f) Oral or written translation can be useful to the teacher in checking and enhancing students' understanding of what has been read. It is best used after several sentences, or a whole paragraph, have been explored. It can be omitted for stories which the class have readily understood or explored intensively in other ways.

Initially, students may find it helpful to use a literal translation or a formula, e.g. *was/were …ing* to translate the imperfect. Students usually discover quite soon that, rather than being a word-for-word process, translation involves rendering Latin into good English, in the appropriate register, so as to convey fully the original writer's meaning. It is the teacher's task to encourage them towards flexibility and the appropriate use of idiomatic phrases.

A variety of methods can be used in classroom translation, e.g.:

- Each sentence is translated by a different student.
- One student translates a paragraph, others suggest improvements.
- Students work in pairs or groups.
- Students contribute suggestions for a collective class translation.

4 *Consolidation*. This is essential to strengthen and maintain students' grasp of story, language and content, and to develop confidence and fluency in reading. Possible activities include:

Listen and hear. Listening, with the book closed, to a reading on the tape or by the teacher. Pause at strategic points to check understanding of the passage. Alternatively, students may mime to a Latin reading.

Latin reading. Preparing to read the story aloud in Latin, with individuals or groups taking different parts or paragraphs. This could be presented to the class or recorded on tape. Choral reading (the class together or in groups) encourages the less confident.

Discussion. Bringing out character, situation, cultural background.

Character analysis. Foretelling the actions or responses of certain characters in certain situations or 'hot-seating' a main character. A well-informed student takes on a character and sits in the centre of the group to be questioned intensively about their motivation and feelings in a given situation.

Language practice. e.g. ask ten quick language questions at the end of a story (vocabulary items, verbs in a particular tense, etc.). Pick out key phrases or sentences illustrating a new language feature; ask students to copy them out, translate them and keep for reference. For further exercises, see pp. 16–17 of this Guide.

Re-telling the story. Telling the story from the viewpoint of one of the characters, taking care to bring out the personality and background details in the narrative.

Developing the story. Searching for clues about how the story will continue.

Background research. Finding out more about the most important places or processes contained in the story. This can lead to a re-telling of the story with full descriptions and explanations.

Illustration. Producing a picture which shows the characters and their locations, or the scene described.

Drama. Making an idiomatic translation of speeches for acting, reading or recording.

Translation. Preparing a group translation of a dramatic scene for acting to the class. Set a polished translation of a prepared passage for homework on a regular basis. Occasionally ask students to revise a story carefully at home; tell them that you will give them three or four sentences from the story to translate in class without any notes or looking up. This is a very precise check on understanding and is quick to set up and mark.

Working on the language. Students gain considerable linguistic understanding from the stories, but the Course provides reinforcement in specific ways.

About the language. When discussing a language feature, the teacher should:

1 Use the examples students have already met in the model sentences and reading passages, in order to organise and consolidate the perceptions they are already forming.

2 Elicit comments on the language feature from students, rather than presenting comment and explanation.

3 Use the practice examples in 'About the language' to make sure that students have understood the explanation. If necessary, supplement these examples by others from the text, from the *Worksheet Masters* or the *Independent Learning Manuals*.

4 Resist the temptation to take the discussion any further, since considerable experience in reading is necessary for students to reach a fuller understanding.

Practising the language. Most of the exercises require students to complete sentences from a pool of words or phrases, and are suitable for both oral and written work. In oral practice, students should respond with the complete Latin sentence, demonstrating their understanding by translating it or answering a question about its meaning.

Other exercises in this section include short stories to be tested by translation or comprehension questions. The level of difficulty is usually slightly below that of the other stories in the Stage.

Additional exercises. The Course is designed with built-in consolidation and students will automatically meet further examples of a feature in later reading passages and exercises. However, teachers should be prepared to give frequent supplementary language practice. Possibilities include:

1 Using a story just read for revising a language feature or a range of features. This ensures that students study words and inflections in the context of a coherent narrative. Possible techniques are:
Oral substitution. e.g. from **portābant** ask for the meanings of **portābat**, **portābam**, progressing to **portāvērunt**, **portant**, then to **portāvit**, **portō** etc. The progression from easy to more difficult questions should be a gradual one. In the example given, first the person is changed, then the tense, then both variables.
Line-by-line questions. Sometimes followed up by a question designed to stress the link between form and function, e.g.:

In line 1, what tense is **ambulābant**? (And how is it translated?)

In line 2, is **dominō** singular or plural? (How does this affect the translation?)

In line 3, find an accusative. (Why is the accusative being used?)

2 Listening to a brief, familiar passage read in Latin, with the textbook closed; students answer comprehension questions, translate sentence by sentence or explain selected phrases. This should be done only with a story just studied or an easy story read previously.

3 Dictation of a brief Latin passage to consolidate grasp of sentence structure, and to relate the spoken to the written word.

4 Memorisation of a short piece of Latin text, e.g. a few model sentences or three or four sentences in a story which contain key vocabulary or sentence structures.

Vocabulary checklist. The words in this list should already be familiar to students. They should be revised and tested. When setting learning homework, discuss different ways of active learning with the class. They may need reminding to cover up the English when testing themselves. However, acquisition and retention of vocabulary depends largely upon the level of interest a story evokes and the frequency and variety of reinforcement activities, e.g.:

1 From a story just read, ask students to give the meaning of individual words or short phrases, *with books open and glossary covered.*

2 *With books shut*, ask a series of questions about the story, setting selected words in a helpful context:

The citizens were **laetī**. What mood were they in?

Each supporter received a **fūstis**. What was that?

Who can show the difference between **sollicitus** and **perterritus**? Basic words can be tested simply: 'What does **scrībit** mean? What is **nāvis**?'

3 Ask students to suggest Latin words on a specific topic, e.g. 'Ten words on the forum before the bell goes – any offers?' or 'Ten pairs of opposites, e.g. **puer/puella**.'

4 Discuss Latin derivatives in English, French, Spanish or Italian. Both the *Worksheet Masters* and the *Independent Learning Manuals* have exercises on derivatives.

Language information. The explanations and exercises in this section are best used as revision and consolidation after students have had considerable experience of all aspects of a feature, e.g. all functions of the dative case. They are not suitable for work on language features which have only recently been introduced. From Stage 8 onwards, teachers will find the tables and exercises helpful in planning additional language practice. Detailed suggestions are made in the Stage commentaries.

The cultural background material

1 Teachers need to vary their treatment of the material, according to the contribution it makes to each Stage. It can be used to:

(a) Introduce a Stage or a story, where the content may need to be explored in advance, e.g. Stage 9 (before **in palaestrā** or **in apodytēriō**).

(b) Follow up the Latin stories, where it extends the content of the stories, e.g. Stages 3, 6, 10.

(c) Accompany the stories, to help students visualise more clearly the setting for the scenes they are reading, e.g. Stages 4, 11.

The simplest and most convenient approach, but by no means the only one, is to ask the class to study the material for homework; then the next lesson can begin with an oral (or written) test of the homework, leading naturally to class discussion and further questions.

In classes where there is a spread of ability, the work given to students will need to be differentiated. For the ablest, the material should provide the entrée to more comprehensive material in class or school library; those for whom reading is difficult will need to have their work tailored to a few key paragraphs. The *Worksheet Masters* offer some exercises for the less able.

2 The illustrations enable students to envisage the Roman setting, and to discover for themselves by observation and deduction more about the Roman world. In the Stage commentaries teachers have been given additional information to assist interpretation of the pictures. This should be transmitted to students only if it seems necessary to aid their understanding and appreciation. Illustrations can be used in a variety of ways.

(a) Individual photographs can help set the scene for a story to be read or acted, e.g. the basilica (pp. 46–7) for the story on p. 44.

(b) A group of pictures can be used to find out the answers to a set of questions, possibly as a preliminary to reading the cultural background material.

(c) Students could enact what would take place in locations illustrated, e.g. in Stages 8 or 9.

(d) The picture essays (e.g. pp. 36–7 and p. 171) can form the basis for independent work by students.

3 Encourage students to compile for later reference a portfolio of the materials they collect or produce themselves. They might select one topic every half term for personal study. It is better for students to study a few topics in depth, rather than to attempt to cover everything.

The personal study need not be restricted to written work. Art work, recording on tape or video, drama and model-making are all effective ways of exploring and expressing knowledge. Even when time is short, students enjoy the opportunity to develop a theme on their own, and it is a good way of encouraging independent learning.

Assessing students' progress

Informal assessment by the teacher is a continuous part of classroom management and lesson planning. It is also essential that formally assessed work is regularly set in class or for homework to provide evidence of individual students' understanding and retention. Occasionally assess students' ability to read Latin aloud; let them see that this is important.

Students should be fully aware of the criteria for assessment of their working attitudes and the work they produce.

This Guide contains attainment tests to be used after every four Stages to assess whether students have understood recent work and consolidated earlier material, or whether they need more work with particular structures. See pp. 95–97.

Graded tests are provided to assess progress at intervals during the Course. See pp. 9, 10.

Lesson planning

There are four key principles in lesson planning, whether you are planning a whole Stage, a series of lessons or a single period.

Motivation. Lessons should have built-in pace and provide regular experience of success for students. A sense of progress and achievement is the single most motivating factor for them.

Developing independence. A teacher promotes independent reading by setting students to work independently or in groups for short periods, and by encouraging them to seek help as required.

Integration. The reading materials are not only a medium for acquiring language, but also the basis for exploring plot, character and the Roman world. This coherence should be constantly reflected in work planned for the class.

Variety. Although reading forms the major part of each lesson, the activities pursued by students, or the work they are set to produce, should be varied to ensure that the lesson has several different phases and momentum is sustained.

An example of a series of three 40-minute lessons is outlined below. It emphasises some of the typical routines which are the basis of most lessons and also indicates how pace and detail will vary according to difficulty or subject matter. The series starts at the end of a Stage so that transition to the following Stage can be demonstrated. The timings given for activities are approximate.

Lesson A

1 Written test on vocabulary checklist of a previous Stage; papers given in (5 mins.).
2 Dramatised readings prepared last time (15 mins.).
3 Introduction to next Stage: study of opening picture to identify theme (5 mins.).
4 Model sentences for next Stage (15 mins.):
   (a) Teacher reads pair of sentences.
   (b) Students translate, with help until correct, using line drawings as clues.
   (c) Repeat with students reading and translating.

Lesson B

1 Teacher comments on test of vocabulary checklist and returns papers (5 mins.).
2 Revision of two to three model sentences from last time (5 mins.).
3 Comprehension exercise on easy new reading passage (15 mins.).
4 Divide next two stories among groups for independent preparation so that each group can tell their story to the rest of the class. Check that each group knows the run-up to their own starting-point. Put directions on board/OHP to save time (15 mins.).

Lesson C

1 Allow time for extra explanation or groups to finish stories (10 mins.).
2 Groups tell stories. Students read some extracts aloud in Latin. They are asked to comment on relevant illustrations (20 mins.).
3 Teacher picks out and discusses examples of the new language feature as preparation for studying the language note next time (10 mins.).
4 Homework: a translation exercise in neat.

Stage commentaries

These notes contain suggestions for planning and teaching Stages 1–12. Each Stage is prefaced by a summary of the content, which is followed by teaching notes for each section in the Stage.

Stories that may be omitted (see p. 11 of this Guide) are marked **.

Teachers should feel free to adapt the advice given in the notes to suit their circumstances, either by using suggestions made in the introduction or by substituting their own ideas.

For further reading on the cultural background material and visual resources consult the bibliography (pp. 100–103).

STAGE 1 Caecilius

Cultural background	Story line	Main language features	Focus of exercises
Pompeii: Caecilius' household; houses in Pompeii.	Caecilius and his household are introduced as they go about their daily business. The dog tries to steal some food while the cook dozes in the kitchen.	• Word order in sentences with **est**. • Word order in sentences without **est**. • Nominative singular.	1 Selection of suitable nominative to complete sentences with **est**. 2 Selection of suitable prepositional phrase to complete sentences with and without **est**.

Introduction

Ask the class to look at the picture on the front cover. Explain that this is a portrait of a real Roman, Caecilius. Encourage them to speculate how we know about him. Find out what students know about Pompeii; they are often well informed about the eruption of Vesuvius and the destruction of the city. Ask them to study the portrait, identifying the features that make up the physiognomy (hooked nose, wrinkled forehead, receding hair, expressive eyes, wart), and guessing the kind of person he might be. Confirm that in Book I they will be reading about him and his household in Pompeii.

Illustrations: front cover and opening page (p. 1)
Close-up of a bronze portrait head found in the house of Lucius Caecilius Iucundus at Pompeii. The whole head appears on p. 9. The stone shaft supporting the head has an inscription identifying it as a man called Lucius; it was put up by a freedman, Felix. It was long considered to be a likeness of Lucius Caecilius Iucundus, the businessman who occupied the house at the time of the eruption and the central figure in Book I. The head is now believed to portray an earlier member of his family, perhaps his father; nevertheless, it is our only clue to our Caecilius' appearance and the line drawings in the Book aim to show a family likeness to this shrewd but kindly face. The head portrayed here is a copy (courtesy *Soprintendenza, Pompeii*) of the original, at present undergoing restoration.

The background is a typical piece of Pompeian wall decoration: a red panel edged with a yellow border reminiscent of embroidery (*Naples, Archaeological Museum*).

Model sentences (pp. 3–5)

New language features. Two basic Latin sentence patterns, one the descriptive statement with **est** (e.g. **Caecilius est pater**), the other the sentence with a verb of action at the end (e.g. **pater in tablīnō scrībit**).

First reading. The line drawings are intended to give students strong clues so that they can work out for themselves the meaning of the Latin sentences. The second and third pages build on the one before. It is important to establish the sentence as the basic unit, and not break it down by analysis at this stage.

p. 3 Read all the sentences in Latin and invite suggestions from the class about their meaning. Re-read and ask for a translation of each.

p. 4 Use leading questions about the drawings to help students identify the characters, locations, etc., e.g.:

Who is in picture 7?

Look at what he is doing. Where do you think he would do that?

Who can now translate the Latin sentence **Caecilius est in tablīnō**?

In looking at the pictures for clues, students will ask questions and make observations about the rooms. Accept these but keep comment brief so that attention is focused on the Latin sentences. After exploring the sentences with the class, ask individuals to read a sentence in Latin and translate it. Handle prepositional phrases such as **in ātriō** as a unit, and encourage students to supply the definite or indefinite article in English as appropriate.

p. 5 This page points up the differing word order of sentences with **est** and those with other verbs. Students may make comments or ask questions. If so, confirm correct observations and help them to form their own conclusions about what they observe. Do not yourself initiate discussion about the language until they have read the story which follows, and are ready for 'About the language' (p. 7).

Students may translate **servus in hortō labōrat** (and similar sentences) as *The slave is in the garden working*. Do not reject this version but encourage alternatives; students will arrive at *The slave is working in the garden* or *The slave works in the garden*.

After this, discuss the line drawings more fully and follow up with work on the cultural background information (pp. 8–13). Among the points to note in the line drawings are:

7 The study opening onto the garden; writing with pen and ink on a papyrus scroll; lamp standard (front right) with book-bin containing furled scrolls behind.

8 The atrium as seen from the study; front door at far end with shrine to lares at left; aperture in roof to admit air, light and water, with pool to collect rainwater below; little furniture.

9 Small dining table, with couches for reclining at dinner.
10 Courtyard garden with colonnade for shelter from sun, plants in tubs and beds, statues, fountain to refresh the air.
11 Cooking pots on charcoal fires, fuel store underneath.
12 Chained guard dog at front door; high kerb.
13 Oil lamp on stand; wax tablets and **stilus** (contrast with 7).

Consolidation. Students could re-read the model sentences for homework. At the beginning of the next lesson give them a few minutes in pairs to refresh their memories, and then ask individuals to read and translate a sentence.

In subsequent lessons, use single sentences as a quick oral drill, and then gradually modify them, e.g. **Caecilius in tablīnō labōrat** (instead of **scrībit**).

Cerberus (p. 6)

Story. Whilst everyone is occupied, Cerberus the dog jumps onto the kitchen table in search of food. Startled by a snore from the sleeping Grumio, he barks and is discovered.

First reading. The story divides naturally into two parts: the household going about its daily business and the scene in the kitchen. Take each paragraph separately as follows:
1 Read it in Latin, clearly and expressively.
2 Give students time to explore the meaning in pairs or groups.
3 Re-read the passage in Latin.
4 Invite suggestions about the meaning. Then develop a translation in groups or as a class.

Consolidation. Divide the class into groups and ask each group to prepare a translation of one of the two paragraphs for reading to the rest of the class. This will bring out minor variations in the English, showing that there is no word-for-word equivalence, and provoking some discussion of alternatives.

Encourage students to comment on the characters and to respond to the story in different ways; interest in character and situation is an important factor in developing reading skill.

Illustration. Mosaic inside the entrance to Caecilius' house. It was common in Pompeian houses of the well-to-do to have a black-and-white mosaic picture just inside the door, which normally stood open in the daytime. Often this showed a watchdog; Caecilius' animal is more relaxed than some and lacks the inscription **cavē canem** found elsewhere (see p. 177).

About the language (p. 7)

New language feature. The different word order in Latin sentences according to whether the verb is **est** or not.

Discussion. The focus here is the sentence as a whole; avoid breaking it down into parts. Take paragraphs 1 and 2 together as the core of this section, and paragraph 3 on its own.

Consolidation. Ask students to find similar examples in the model sentences or the story.

Practising the language (p. 7)

Exercise 1. Practice in the structure of sentences with **est**.
Exercise 2. Completion of sentence with appropriate prepositional phrase.

Note. Encourage students to select the option which makes the best sense. Writing out a complete Latin sentence and its translation correctly, however easy, reinforces confidence and grasp of the language.

Cultural background material (pp. 8–13)

Content. Students are introduced to the members of the household and the house in which they lived and worked.

Discussion. The material can be taken in two parts, starting with the sections on Caecilius and Metella. Students could be asked to read this for homework after they meet members of the household in the model sentences. The class discussion that follows might include:
1 The position and character of Pompeii as a cosmopolitan port and fashionable residential town.
2 How the port, the city and the surrounding countryside contributed to Caecilius' business interests.
3 What qualities Caecilius, as a successful businessman, would look for in his wife.
4 The importance of slaves in a household.

The information about the house could be approached by a study of the pictures. The line drawings (p. 4), of the **tablīnum**, the **ātrium**, the garden and the view through the house between the front door and the garden, could be compared with the photographic material on pp. 12–13. Follow this by reading the text. Discussion points:
1 How we can reconstruct Pompeian houses and gardens on the basis of archaeological findings.
2 Why Pompeian houses were designed to look inward.
3 The amenities which were available, such as heating, lighting and water.

Further information. The basis of our knowledge about Caecilius is 153 wax tablets containing his business records, which were discovered in 1875 in a strong-box in his house. They include records of a loan, sales of timber and land, the rent for a laundry and for land leased from the town council, and the auction of linen on behalf of an Egyptian merchant. His normal commission was 2%.

The **praenōmen** (personal name) of Caecilius' son, Quintus, is supported by inscriptions. The names attributed to the rest of the household are invented.

Caecilius' house (Regio V, Insula I. 26) is not currently accessible, but visible from the street are the mosaic of the dog (p. 6) and the view shown on p. 12 (top right), with some patches of wall-painting. The contents of the house are currently in store, either in Pompeii or in the Naples Archaeological Museum.

Illustrations

p. 8 • The front of Caecilius' house on the Via Vesuvio, the northern part of Stabiae Street (plan, p. 34). Like many prosperous houses it has, on each side of the tall, imposing front door, shops which might have been leased out or managed by the owner's slaves or freedmen. The adjoining house seen further up the street, to the left, also belonged to Caecilius.

• Caecilius leased a laundry from the town council, but we do not know where it was. The one illustrated is the laundry of Stephanus in the Via dell' Abbondanza. We see a large tank for washing cloth in the front of the shop. More were installed in the yard at the back, and drying and bleaching (using urine) were carried out on the flat roof. A tunic cost 1 denarius to launder.

• Map of the Bay of Naples.

p. 9 • The bronze head from Caecilius' house (see Introduction, p. 21).

• A carbonised tablet from Caecilius' archive, with a drawing of another showing writing.

• Examples of Roman coins: sestertius of Caligula marking the death of his mother Agrippina; denarius of Augustus celebrating the capture of Egypt; aureus of Sulla with head of Venus (*Rome, Museo Nazionale Romano*). The basic denomination was the as, a bronze coin. The sestertius was worth 4 asses, the denarius 16 asses and the aureus 100 asses.

• A wood and bronze strong-box similar to the one in which Caecilius kept his tablets (*Naples, Archaeological Museum*).

p. 10 • Marble statue of Eumachia, with traces of paint on the hair. It was found in the building she financed, which has been identified as the Clothworkers' Guildhall.

- Portrait head of a woman, showing side view of a hairstyle similar to Metella's (*Naples, Archaeological Museum*).
- Two pinheads from the bone pins that were used to control elaborate hairstyles. The women's heads on these pinheads give further evidence of hair styling. About AD 100 (*British Museum*).

p. 11
- Diagram showing the typical features of the Roman atrium house. These houses, with many individual variations, are common in Pompeii; there are also smaller houses and flats.
  - Façade of the House of the Wooden Partition at Herculaneum, shown because of its preservation. Note that the doors open directly onto the pavement, and the windows are small and high up. The house is faced with painted stucco. The house further down the street, built over the pavement, is timber framed and contained a number of separate flats.

p. 12
- The atrium of Caecilius' house, showing the impluvium, the mosaic floor and a little painted plaster on the walls. We also see (on the left) the space called an **āla** (wing) that often opens off an atrium, the tablinum and garden behind. To the left of the tablinum is the pedestal which supported the bronze head (pp. 1, 9).
  - The atrium of the House of the Menander, one of the grandest houses in Pompeii. The vista shown was contrived to impress visitors and passers-by, who would be able to see through the open front door. The walls of the entrance hall are partly visible at either side. In the atrium beyond, we can see the **compluvium**, the opening in the roof through which water fell into the impluvium below. Behind, two columns frame the tablinum with the peristylium beyond; a corridor to the left allowed access to the garden at times when the master desired privacy in the tablinum, which could be closed off by a curtain. In the far distance are some of the rooms opening off the peristyle.
  - A lararium. Statuettes of gods and offerings of food, wine and flowers would have been placed in this little shrine; its back wall would have been decorated with pictures of the household gods (lares and penates) and, often, of protective snakes.

p. 13
- Caecilius' tablinum. It had a rather plain mosaic floor and painted walls, with pictures of nymphs and satyrs on white rectangles against coloured panels designed to suggest hanging tapestries.
  - The walls of gardens were often painted with trees, flowers, trellises, birds and fountains, to supplement the real garden and give the illusion that it was larger. Example from the House of Venus. See also p. 32.

- A small, well-preserved peristyle in Herculaneum (House of the Relief of Telephus). Notice the decorative carved marble discs hanging between the columns. Garlands of flowers and foliage would be draped between these and the columns on festive occasions.

p. 14 Examples of Roman jewellery of the period: a gold snake bracelet, cast solid and finely chased; a snake ring; a pair of emerald cluster earrings; and one of a pair of hollow gold ball earrings (*British Museum*).

Suggested activities

1 Draw side by side plans of a Pompeian house and a house offered by a local estate agent. Label the rooms. Write briefly about the differences you notice, saying which one you prefer and why.
2 Using a picture from Stage 1 as a centre-piece, write an estate agent's advertisement for a Pompeian villa, describing its amenities.
3 In a shoe-box, make a model of a Pompeian house based on the plan on p. 11. Decorate the walls and add furniture. What do you notice when you look through the front door of your finished house? (This activity is motivating, but time-consuming and more suitable for young students.)
4 *Worksheet Master* 1.4 combines revision of the rooms in the Roman house with English derivations.

Vocabulary checklist

Students will already be familiar with all or most of these words, since they will have occurred several times in the material. It is helpful to ask them to recall the context in which they met a word because the association will often fix it in their minds. Discussion of derivations is valuable for extending students' vocabulary in English and other modern languages and will also reinforce their grasp of Latin.

The checklist can be used for oral practice, with the English covered up, or set to be revised for homework. Frequent short checks and tests, often in the context of a story, are much more effective than one comprehensive test at the end of term. The *Worksheet Masters* and the *Independent Learning Manual* contain vocabulary exercises for every Stage.

Note. Checklist words are marked with an asterisk (*) in the vocabulary on pp. 191–9.

STAGE 2 in vīllā

Cultural background	Story line	Main language features	Focus of exercises
Pompeii: daily life and food.	Dinner party. Grumio enjoys himself as Caecilius and his guest sleep off their meal.	• Nominative and accusative singular. • Sentence pattern NOMINATIVE + ACCUSATIVE + VERB.	1 Completion of sentence with suitable noun, verb or phrase. 2 Completion of sentence with suitable verb. 3 Story for translation.

Opening page (p. 15)

Illustration. Reconstructed bedroom from a villa at Boscoreale, near Pompeii, owned by Publius Fannius Synistor, a very wealthy man. The walls are decorated with panels drawn from theatre scenes of comedy, tragedy and satyr plays (*New York, Metropolitan Museum of Art*).

Model sentences (pp. 16–19)

New language feature. The accusative is introduced in the context of a common sentence pattern: NOMINATIVE + ACCUSATIVE + VERB.

New vocabulary. amīcus, salūtat, spectat, parātus, gustat, anxius, laudat, vocat.

First reading. Introduce the situation briefly, e.g. 'A friend (**amīcus**) is visiting Caecilius.' Then take the first pair of sentences as follows:
Sentence 1. Read in Latin, then ask who is in the picture and where he is.
Sentence 2. Read in Latin, then explore the situation, e.g. 'Who is in the picture with Caecilius? What is he doing?' Read the Latin sentence again and ask for the meaning. Encourage a variety of meanings for **salūtat**, e.g: *says hello to, greets.* The main thing is to establish the correct grammatical relationship between **amīcus** and **Caecilium**. If students ask, 'Isn't his name Caecilius?', confirm that they should continue to use the form Caecilius; do not enter into explanations yet.

Repeat the process with each pair of sentences as far as 9 and 10. Most students are quick to understand the new sentence pattern.

Run through sentences 1–10 quickly again, with pairs of students for each pair of sentences. Students should read their sentences aloud and translate them.

Then follow the same process with sentences 11–20.

Consolidation. Re-use the pairs of sentences for quick oral drill in the next lesson or two, to reinforce the natural English word order for translating the second sentence.

mercātor (p. 20)

Story. Caecilius is working in the study when a merchant calls for dinner. Grumio keeps them waiting.

First reading. This simple story comes to life for the class if first read aloud in Latin by the teacher with good phrasing, dramatic interpretation and well-controlled pace. It is important to:
1 Teach the class to look at new words in their context first, only consulting the vocabulary list when necessary.
2 Ask leading questions to elicit the meaning of a paragraph or group of sentences, and encourage a range of different interpretations before a formal version is agreed.
3 Follow up hints on character and attitude (e.g. Grumio's cheerful and extrovert nature, Caecilius' irritation) and information about the daily work of Caecilius and Grumio.

Consolidation. The class should acquire a sound grasp of story, language and cultural content. Re-reading should be as varied as possible, and might include:
1 A group attempt to achieve the closest and most natural English version.
2 A re-enactment of the story.
3 Isolating some of the sentences containing the accusative and asking their meaning.
4 Inviting speculation about what will follow the end of the story.
   Refer students to the description of Caecilius' business interests (p. 8) and daily life, including the picture of bankers (p. 23). For illustrations relating to Grumio's work, see the model sentences, pp. 18–19 and pp. 21, 26.

in triclīniō (p. 20)

Story. The dinner served by Grumio is a success, as is the after-dinner entertainment. When Caecilius and his guest take a nap, Grumio makes himself at home.

First reading. Students will be able to visualise this story if it is linked with the information about meals and Roman food (pp. 24–5), which could be read for homework in advance.
   This story is best handled in sections. Encourage students to develop the habit of using the context to establish the sense of a passage, returning later to clarify details.

Consolidation. Use various ways of re-reading the text (see Introduction, pp. 15–16). Ask the class to comment on Caecilius' praise of Grumio after his earlier reprimand, and Grumio's opportunistic behaviour.

About the language (p. 21)

New language feature. The difference in function and form between nominative and accusative. Discussion of declensions is postponed until Stage 3.

Discussion. Start by putting one pair of the model sentences on the board or OHP (e.g. **Caecilius est in ātriō. amīcus Caecilium salūtat.**).

Teacher: **Caecilius** appears in both sentences, but there is a difference in the ways in which he appears in the Latin. Can you point out the difference?

Answer: In one he is **Caecilius**, in the other **Caecilium**.

Teacher: Both these Latin words mean **Caecilius** but they have different forms. **Caecilius** is called the NOMINATIVE case and **Caecilium** is called the ACCUSATIVE case [write them up]. Look again at the sentence **amīcus Caecilium salūtat** and notice how it is translated.

Then put up other sentences with accusatives (including endings in **-am**, **-um**, **-em**) and invite comment. Observations usually include:

1 The nominative shows someone who does something.
2 The accusative shows a person who has something done to them.
3 The accusative ends in **-m**.
4 The Latin accusative is in the middle, but the English translation has the corresponding word at the end.

Then study 'About the language'. Add further examples if necessary, always in complete sentences and using familiar words. Concentrate on using the terms NOMINATIVE and ACCUSATIVE and their characteristic endings, rather than introducing additional terms such as *subject* and *object*. If students themselves use these terms, confirm that they are correct, but continue to use the case names.

Consolidation. Go back to the stories on p. 20, and ask students to pick out nominatives and accusatives. For instance, taking **in triclīniō**: 'What case is **coquum** in line 6? In **coquus ancillam spectat** in line 13, which word is nominative?' Sometimes ask for a translation of the sentence under discussion, to remind students of the grammatical relationship shown by the case names.

Illustration. Peacock wall-painting (*Naples, Archaeological Museum*).

Practising the language (p. 22)

Exercise 1. Practice in the structure of a simple sentence. Students use the sense and structure of the sentence to insert the missing item (noun, verb or prepositional phrase).

Exercise 2. Completion of sentence with a verb, selected according to sense. Incidental reinforcement of accusative. In example **i**, **cēnam** and **canem** may cause confusion. The English derivative *canine* may help.

Exercise 3. Story. A friend visits Grumio and helps himself to food before Grumio appears. Introduce a discussion of English idiom by comparing translations of **amīcus cibum cōnsūmit** (*The friend eats the food / The friend is eating the food*). Ask the class which is the more natural translation.

Worksheet Master 2.3 practises the use of the nominative and accusative in the context of a story.

Cultural background material (pp. 23–5)

Content. A brief description of daily life including meals, dress and the **salūtātiō** (morning visit).

Discussion. Material is best introduced where it relates to the stories, e.g. p. 23 with **mercātor** (p. 20), and pp. 24–5 with **in triclīniō** (p. 20).

Further information. Informal family meals including **ientāculum** (*breakfast*) and **prandium** (*lunch*) were eaten standing or sitting; reclining on one's elbow was a formality generally practised at the **cēna** (*dinner*), especially when guests were present. *Worksheet Master* 2.6 includes some Roman dishes and accounts of dinner parties by Martial, *Epigrams* XI.52, and Pliny, *Letters* I.15.

The times of meals and work during the Roman day were earlier than ours. This information could provoke discussion of the effect of the Mediterranean climate on daily life then and now, and the absence of strong artificial light in the ancient world. The use of sun-dials (see illustration, p. 135) might raise questions about how accurately and how often the Romans needed to tell the time. The sun-dial picture can be used to elicit the point that an hour (i.e. one-twelfth of the period of daylight) could be 45 minutes in midwinter, 75 in midsummer.

Peacocks (illustrations, pp. 19, 21) were popular in the Roman world not only as food and wall decoration, but also as live ornaments in gardens.

Illustrations

p. 23 • Roman dressed in toga. Honorific marble statue from Herculaneum (*Naples, Archaeological Museum*).
   • Relief of about AD 230 showing two bankers, the one on the left with a scroll and the one on the right with a money-bag. Someone is bringing them a bag of money on his shoulder. The counter has a protective barrier at the right side (*Rome, Museo Nazionale Romano*).

p. 24 Carbonised loaf of bread found in Pompeii (*Naples, Archaeological Museum*).

p. 25 • Bowl of eggs found in Pompeii (*Naples, Archaeological Museum*).
   • A popular subject for a dining-room floor was food, particularly
     fish. Detail from a larger mosaic depicting a fight between an
     octopus and a lobster, from a triclinium in the House of the Faun
     in Pompeii (*Naples, Archaeological Museum*).
   • Wall-painting of a larder (*Naples, Archaeological Museum*).
   • Bowl of fruit in the villa of the Poppaei family at Oplontis. Note
     the artist's skill in showing the transparency of glass.
   • Basket of figs in the dining-room of the villa at Oplontis.
p. 26 Cooking pots and trivets in the kitchen of the House of the Vettii,
   Pompeii.

Suggested activities

1 You are a baker and a **cliēns** of Caecilius. Write an account of your
   morning visit to Caecilius' house. Include a description of your
   surroundings and the conversations that occur.
2 Design an invitation to a Roman dinner party, with the menu and
   description of the entertainments (for details see *Worksheet Masters* 2.6
   and 2.7).
3 Sample some Roman dishes or simulate a Roman dinner party. For easy
   recipes see *The Roman Cookery of Apicius*, trans. J. Edwards.
4 Look at the examples of wall-paintings in the first four Stages. Then
   design a simple wall panel and colour appropriately, possibly on
   computer.
5 Make an illustrated diary of a day in the life of Caecilius and the same
   for Metella. Set them side by side so that they can be compared.

STAGE 3 negōtium

Cultural background	Story line	Main language features	Focus of exercises
Pompeii: town life and business.	Caecilius goes to work in the forum. Celer paints a mural in Caecilius' villa. Caecilius visits Pantagathus, the barber. He buys a pretty slave-girl from Syphax, the slave-dealer.	Nominative and accusative of 1st, 2nd and 3rd declensions.	1 Selection of suitable verb. 2 Selection of nominative or accusative.

Opening page (p. 27)

Illustration. This wall-painting of an unidentified harbour, found at Stabiae, introduces the theme of commerce. A pier encloses the harbour, where ships stand at anchor. In the foreground are small fishing-boats. An angler with rod is perched on a rock (bottom left). Visible along the harbour side are: colonnades with marble ornaments hanging between the columns, fortifications (on right), and commemorative pillars carrying statues of prominent citizens (*Naples, Archaeological Museum*).

**in forō (p. 28)

Story. Caecilius is in the forum, conducting his business as a banker, and meets Celer the wall-painter and Pantagathus the barber. Syphax the slave-dealer is angry because a merchant misses an appointment.

First reading. Read the story aloud dramatically so that students gain an impression of the range of people and occurrences in the forum. Refer to the line drawing to introduce the characters and their surroundings, and use a series of quick questions to keep the pace of interpretation brisk.

Consolidation. In discussion, establish the forum as the centre of social and business life in Pompeii. Draw on students' knowledge of Caecilius' business interests as an **argentārius** (Stage 1, pp. 8–9). This is a good story for students to practise reading aloud, to develop confidence and accuracy in pronunciation.

Illustration. The line drawing shows the forum as it would have looked before the earthquake of AD 62: a large paved space, lined on both sides by colonnades with an upper floor and Vesuvius pre-eruption behind. The Temple of Jupiter can be seen (centre), flanked by arches with honorific statues of the emperor's family.

pictor (p. 29)

Story. Celer is welcomed by Quintus and taken by Metella to the dining-room, where he paints a mural which meets with Caecilius' approval.

First reading. Divide the story into two sections, lines 1–7 and 8–end. After reading the first section aloud in Latin, use comprehension questions with the whole group (cf. p. 14 above). Then translate the second section in pairs initially, referring to the picture, followed by group comments and comparisons.

Language. Students have already met prepositional phrases (**in ātriō, in vīllā**) and this story introduces more (**ad vīllam, ad triclīnium, ad iānuam**). From hearing you reading the Latin, students should naturally handle these phrases as complete units and not split them into separate words.

Adjectives have so far been used predicatively (**coquus est laetus**) and are now being used attributively (**magnus leō, magnum fūstem**). This should cause students no difficulty in understanding and should not be analysed until Stages 14 and 18, where there are notes on adjectives.

Consolidation. Different students could re-read the sentences concerned with the different characters: pictor, Metella, canis, etc.

Further information. Celer is typical of Campanian artists of the period who reproduced Greek subjects, often from Greek originals, but showed skills greater than those of mere copyists. Here Hercules is engaged on the first of his Twelve Labours, overcoming the Nemean lion. For the method of painting frescos, see p. 73 of this Guide.

Illustrations. The three small pictures (*Naples, Archaeological Museum*) are chosen to illustrate a range of popular themes. The shepherd boy has pointed ears because he is a satyr. Cupids are commonly found engaged in everyday activities ranging from wine-making to chariot-racing. The poet is holding a rolled-up scroll with a label, and is wearing a garland.

tōnsor (p. 30)

Story. While Caecilius waits his turn at the barber's, a poet recites a rude rhyme which so infuriates Pantagathus that an accident occurs.

First reading. Read the story aloud in as dramatic a manner as possible and ascertain, by general questioning, how much students have understood. Some may have grasped the situation immediately. The word order VERB + NOMINATIVE, e.g. **respondet Pantagathus**, is used here for the first time, but needs no comment.

Comprehension questions. Use these after the whole passage has been read and when you think students are ready to tackle them successfully. This is the first time they occur in students' text, and they may serve as a guide to teachers for writing questions for other passages. The answers and mark scheme are given below. You may find that students give unexpected but valid answers, and credit should be given for these.

		Marks
1	The barber/Pantagathus.	1
2	He is trimming a beard/the old man's beard.	1
3	A poet.	1
4	The poet's (rude) verse.	1
5	The barber does not smile/is angry.	1
6	He cuts him.	1
7	Caecilius gets up and leaves the shop.	2
	He is scared that the barber will cut him.	1
8	**senex novāculam intentē spectat.**	1
	TOTAL	10

Consolidation. If students have managed the comprehension questions well, there is no need for further consolidation. If not, set part of the story for a written translation.

Further information. Pantagathus the barber has a name suggesting Greek origins. At this time Romans were generally clean shaven and visited the barber during the morning, so his shop became the centre of news and gossip. In the line drawing he is shown using a folding razor of Roman design. The poet's visit is a reminder that the customary way for writers to draw public attention to their work was by reciting or reading it aloud.

vēnālīcius (p. 31)

Story. Caecilius seeks out the slave-dealer to buy a new slave and returns home with a pretty slave-girl whose arrival provokes mixed reactions.

First reading. Discuss the line drawing and establish that Syphax deals in slaves from overseas. Then explore the story with comprehension questions, e.g.:
1 In the first paragraph find the word which suggests where Syphax has come from.
2 Why, in line 9, does Syphax call for wine? Some students will see this as a way of softening up Caecilius, others as a chance to introduce Melissa.
3 In lines 13–14, what are Melissa's skills, according to Syphax? Some students may render **Melissa cēnam optimam coquit** (line 13) as *Melissa cooks very good dinners* or *Melissa cooks dinner very well*. Such answers reveal that they have understood the meaning of the text. Guide the class towards *Melissa cooks a very good dinner* by asking 'What kind of dinner does Melissa cook?'.

Consolidation. Translation of this story enables the class to discuss the most appropriate English for such phrases as **salvē, Syphāx!** spoken by a businessman; **ancilla Caecilium dēlectat**; and **ēheu!** This is the best story to act out in this Stage.

The last paragraph usually provokes a lively discussion of the characters and their attitudes.

Additional information. Syphax, an imaginary character like Celer and Pantagathus, is an astute Syrian who makes his living in the slave trade, bringing skilled as well as manual labourers to the Italian market. Because slaves were less frequently available from military conquest during this period, prices were high (see p. 53).

Illustrations. Shears of the kind illustrated were used instead of scissors (*Museum of London*). Troublesome slaves might be shackled to prevent escape (*Cambridge, Museum of Archaeology and Anthropology*).

About the language (p. 32)

New language feature. Nouns are tabulated in declensions (nominative and accusative singular of 1st, 2nd and 3rd declensions only).

Discussion. Note the forms, and stress that knowledge of one example within a declension is the key to all or most of the others.

Consolidation. Follow up with more oral revision of the nominative and accusative cases:
1   Give students an English sentence and ask them which word is in the nominative/accusative.
2   Using one of the Stage 3 stories, ask students to pick out nominatives and accusatives which they have already met in context. For instance, in **vēnālīcius**: 'What case is **servum** in line 6? Which word is nominative in **Caecilius Melissam emit** in line 15?' Occasionally ask for a translation to remind students of the function of the two cases.
3   With p. 32 open, and using only the examples provided, ask students to give the Latin for a word in an English sentence, e.g.:
I entered *the shop*.
The merchant bought *the slave*.

Illustration. Golden oriole (*Naples, Archaeological Museum*).

Practising the language (p. 33)

Exercise 1. Selection of verb according to sense.
Exercise 2. Selection of nominative or accusative singular.

Cultural background material (pp. 33–7)

Content. An overview of the layout of Pompeii, its main features and its links with the rest of the Roman Empire.

Discussion. Use the pictures in this Stage and on pp. 43, 65, 107, 125 and

146 (and any other available material) to help students identify the main features (forum, theatre, amphitheatre, baths, streets, houses, tenements and civic monuments) and locate them on the plan on p. 34. Their social functions should be emphasised. If appropriate, encourage students to imagine Caecilius or Grumio showing a friend round the town. Students may need help in appreciating the size of the town. At 66 hectares, the town was about half a mile square. It is worth comparing this measurement with a local park, the school grounds or some other familiar space.

Discussion points might include:

1 Comparison with a modern town, highlighting similarities (large sports buildings, prevalence of graffiti) and differences (volume of traffic, absence of street names).

2 Amenities, including entertainments, open spaces, transport, home lighting, water supply, transmission of news, cooking facilities, keeping warm or cool, finding someone's address.

Further information. The nationalities of Syphax, Pantagathus and Celer illustrate how cosmopolitan Pompeii was because of its mercantile contacts with east and west, and because its development included occupation by Etruscans, Greeks and Samnites before the Romans. The people of Pompeii thrived on trade and industry, and enjoyed a comfortable, even luxurious, lifestyle. Civic pride was strong and was expressed in public buildings, statues and inscriptions, and in the civic deity, Venus Pompeiana. Many public buildings were erected by individuals at their own expense. Most buildings had been badly damaged by the earthquake in AD 62. Some, including the Temples of Venus and Jupiter, were still in need of restoration; others, including the amphitheatre, had been restored; private houses were repaired to an unprecedented standard of luxury; and a new and very large bath complex, the Central Baths, had been started.

Illustrations

p. 33 A status symbol for the Romans was a seaside villa on the Bay of Naples. This small landscape suggests how tightly packed villas could be. It is a wall-painting in the lavishly decorated tablinum of Marcus Lucretius Fronto in Pompeii.

p. 34 The photograph shows stepping-stones worn with use, ruts from wheeled vehicles and the height of the pavement on the far side.

p. 35 • Fountain in the Street of the Shops (Via dell' Abbondanza). Notice also the house preserved up to the first floor.

• Bakery in Pompeii with two corn mills. Only the conical bottom stone remains from the front mill. The one behind is almost complete. The corn was fed into an opening in the top of the movable stone, which was shaped to sit on top of the bottom stone and turned by a slave or animal by means of a handle fitted into the socket on the side, just visible in the photograph. The flour ran out between the two stones and collected on the circular platform beneath.

p. 36 Stabiae Street looking south. The Stabiae Gate is visible at the end of the street. There is a water tower at front left. Note the well-preserved stepping-stones.

pp. 36–7 *Streets of Pompeii*. Clockwise starting from mid-left:
- She-goat shop sign of dairy near the forum.
- Cast of shop shutters, formed by pouring concrete into the space left by rotted wood.
- Street corner in older part of town, where streets are not arranged on a regular grid pattern. It shows how extra space could be obtained for the upstairs rooms. This house was a brothel.
- Professionally painted electoral slogans. Exterior plaster walls were commonly painted red at the bottom and white at the top.
- Bar in Via dell' Abbondanza, with amphorae stacked in corner. Let into the counter are three pottery jars to contain the food on offer, in one of which the excavators found 1,611 coins of low denominations, the last day's takings. Painted on the wall behind is a lararium with Mercury, the god associated with profit (and thieves) at the far left, holding a purse.
- Wall-painting from a small bar near the Forum on the north side, not far from Caecilius' house.
- Asellina's bar on opposite side of street, with amphorae stacked in corner. The excavators found the bronze vessels still on the counter.

p. 38 Mercury, distinguished by his winged hat and characteristic herald's staff. One of five gods painted above a shop doorway in Via dell' Abbondanza.

Suggested activities

1 Give each student an outline plan of the town (see *Worksheet Master* 3.6). They should fill in the key features (forum, theatres, amphitheatre, palaestra, Caecilius' house, Stabian Baths, Forum Baths, main shopping area, sea gate, other gates). Alternatively, use the OHP for a similar joint exercise with the whole class, or use the simple exercise set in *Worksheet Master* 3.6.

2 Ask groups of students to write or record a visitor's guide to Pompeii, or design a travel poster or website, researching to amplify the material in the Stage or adding material from subsequent Stages.

STAGE 4 in forō

Cultural background	Story line	Main language features	Focus of exercises
The forum at Pompeii; finance and the law courts.	Caecilius lends money to a Greek merchant, Hermogenes; he does not repay the debt and is taken to court by Caecilius.	1st and 2nd person singular present, including **sum, es**.	1 Selection of suitable verb in 1st or 2nd person singular. 2 Story for translation.

Opening page (p. 39)

Illustration. View of forum seen through arch on eastern side of Temple of Jupiter (opposite view from that on p. 28). Part of the temple can be seen on the right. The brick buildings at the far end are the municipal offices. In the foreground, two stone blocks prevent wheeled traffic from entering the forum. The arch which frames the picture is made of brick-faced concrete but was originally faced with marble.

Model sentences (pp. 40–2)

New language feature. The 1st and 2nd person singular of the present tense. Familiar characters state in the 1st person who they are and what they are doing. They then answer questions posed to them in the 2nd person.

New vocabulary. ego, tū, quid, quis.

First reading. This presents little difficulty because the pictures give strong clues and there is little new vocabulary. Suggested procedure:

1 Teacher reads Grumio's statement (1) in Latin.
2 Teacher says, 'Grumio is speaking. What does he say?' If necessary, act out the statement, emphasising **ego**.
3 Encourage use of the immediate present, e.g. *What are you selling*? (10), rather than *What do you sell*?
4 After the meaning has been elicited, give other parts to individuals or groups. Ask them to read each pair of sentences aloud in Latin and then translate.

Note. ego and **tū** have been inserted in these sentences to aid students. They are gradually phased out in the Stages which follow.

Consolidation. A mime game is useful here. Students take it in turns to mime actions and the class guesses who they are or what they are doing (e.g. **tū es poēta** or **tū versum recitās**). If the class cannot guess, the student has to tell them (e.g. **ego sum poēta** or **ego versum recitō**).

Hermogenēs (p. 43)

Story. Caecilius lends money to Hermogenes, a Greek merchant. He requires the transaction to be recorded on a wax tablet with the imprint of the merchant's seal. Hermogenes does not repay the loan.

First reading. Read the story at one sitting, leaving students eager to find out what happens next.

The 1st and 2nd person singular crop up naturally in the dialogue. Any further comment on the language should be postponed until study of the language note. If **ego pecūniam quaerō** (line 5) causes difficulty, remind students that when Caecilius went to the port to see Syphax (p. 31) we were told **Caecilius servum quaerit**. A reminder of the context of a word's previous occurrence is far more effective than looking up the word in the general vocabulary.

At the end of the story invite speculation about what will happen in court. In order to respond, and to understand the implications of what Caecilius says in line 10 (**ego cēram habeō. tū ānulum habēs?**), students will need to know about the Roman practice of recording business transactions on wax tablets. See 'Further information' below.

Consolidation. Follow up with a dramatic reading, or recapitulate when introducing the next story, or postpone consolidation until **in basilicā** has been read and the incident can be dramatised in its entirety.

Further information. Seals were commonly carried as rings, as illustrated on p. 44. Wax tablets recording business transactions (illustrated on pp. 9 and 47) were usually bound together in a set of three (i.e. six sides) as follows:

Front cover. Plain wood with title inscribed in ink.

Sides 2 and 3. Agreement or receipt in full, engraved in wax.

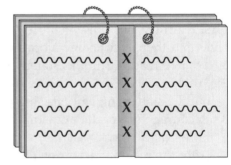

Side 4. Special leaf for signatures, with a fairly wide groove down the centre. The two tablets were tied together down the middle with string, and fastened along the groove with wax. The participants and witnesses would each press their seal into the wax and sign their name across the leaf, using both sides of the groove. In the illustration above, **X** represents the seal.

Side 5. Summary, giving brief details and names from the main text, possibly for reference, to enable the main text to remain sealed, or in case of loss.

Back cover. Usually plain wood. The complete triptych was then bound round the outside.

Caecilius' surviving business records, the main source for our knowledge about him, are of this type.

Illustration. Looking towards the arch where the previous photograph (p. 39) was taken. In front of the row of shops stood a colonnade which was roofed to give protection from the sun. The row of pedestals inside the colonnade would have supported statues of prominent citizens. The columns have been partly reconstructed in brickwork in modern times.

in basilicā (p. 44)

Play. Caecilius takes Hermogenes to court and wins his case on the evidence of the wax tablet and the signet ring.

First reading. Set the scene and establish the court procedures by asking comprehension questions on lines 2–11. Then tell students to explore the meaning in groups of five in preparation for assuming the characters of narrator, judge, Caecilius, Hermogenes and his friend.

Check students' understanding of the meaning and help them to envisage the scene and reflect on the characters by asking, e.g.:

What do you think Caecilius does at line 26?

Why does Hermogenes say **ēheu!** in line 27? How loudly do you think he says it?

What is Hermogenes doing in line 29 when Caecilius says **ecce!**? Why?

What does the judge do in line 30 before saying **ānulus rem probat**?

Consolidation. Once students have an understanding of the story, draw attention to the illustrations of the basilica (p. 46), and the trial and writing tablet (p. 47).

Paired groups could then perform the play, one in English, followed by one in Latin. The rest of the class could supply the reactions of the onlookers in court. A final version could be recorded on tape or video.

Worksheet Master 4.3, which provides a check on students' grasp of the story, could be set for homework.

Illustrations

p. 44 Clockwise from left:
- Enlarged image of peridot (semi-precious stone) seal engraved with horse (*Cambridge, Fitzwilliam Museum*).
- Seal ring made in gold without jewels (*Victoria and Albert Museum*).
- An amethyst with Medusa's head (*British Museum*).
- A cornelian showing Hygeia, goddess of health (*British Museum*).
- An onyx showing a warship (*British Museum*).

About the language (p. 45)

New language feature. 1st and 2nd person singular of the present tense.

Discussion. Ask students what they have noticed in the model sentences.

Most will mention **ego** and **tū**; some will have spotted the new verb endings. See what progress they make with the formulation of rules; then proceed with the language note.

Consolidation. Follow the initial reading with oral practice of other familiar verbs. Retain **ego** and **tū**, or use a noun as subject, for the time being. When students appear confident, follow up with further oral practice in the 1st and 2nd person with the subject omitted.

Practising the language (pp. 46–7)

Exercise 1. Selection of suitable verb to match the subject in 1st or 2nd person.
***Exercise 2.* Story. Grumio comes home drunk and is frightened by the mural of a lion in the dining-room.

Illustrations

p. 46 As can be seen from the air photograph on p. 51 of Book I, the basilica was vast. Its roof timbers were supported on 28 brick pillars surrounding the central space. Like the walls, these were covered in stucco and painted to look like marble. The rectangular object is the base of an equestrian statue.

p. 47 • Detail of a painting from Pompeii which shows the judgment of Solomon or a parallel story. Two soldiers watch as a woman kneels before a judge on the tribunal. On either side of him is an adviser. (*Naples, Archaeological Museum*)

• Wax tablet as described on p. 40 of this Guide (*Naples, Archaeological Museum*).

Cultural background material (pp. 48–51)

Content. The physical appearance of the forum and the range and importance of the activities which occurred there.

Discussion. A single location for state ceremonial, law, religion, administration, business and daily shopping will be a strange concept for many students. Discussion of the question, 'Is there a modern equivalent?' will enable them to draw on their own experience of village green, town market square or urban shopping precinct, and to examine the significance of the Pompeian evidence more closely for similarities.

Illustrations

p. 48 • Part of colonnade on west side of forum. The lower storey is Doric, the upper Ionic – which, following Greek tradition, is more slender.

• Line drawing based on a frieze showing scenes in the forum, found in the atrium of the house of Julia Felix. Photographs of other scenes from the same frieze are on pp. 49 and 142. (*Naples, Archaeological Museum*).

p. 49 Equestrian statue (restored). This comes from Herculaneum. No statues were found in the forum at Pompeii, either because they had been removed for restoration after the earthquake of AD 62 or because they were recovered by survivors after the eruption (*Naples, Archaeological Museum*).

p. 50 Scroll of plant forms inhabited by birds. Fine decoration carved in marble on the doorway of the Clothworkers' Guildhall.

p. 51 The air photograph of the forum is surrounded by details of some of the principal buildings. The notes below are numbered to match the photograph. Those that refer also to the surrounding illustrations have headings printed in bold type.

1 **Temple of Jupiter**, flanked by two triumphal arches.

2 **The market hall** had little shops along its walls inside and out, with the fish market at the back. In the middle of the central court-yard were a water tank and a small structure with a domed roof.

3 Temple of the Lares of Pompeii, possibly built in expiation after the earthquake of AD 62.

4 **Temple of the Emperors**, dedicated to the cult of the most recent emperor. At the time of the eruption in AD 79 this was Vespasian, who had died two months earlier.

5 Eumachia's Clothworkers' Guildhall. This headquarters of the guild of fullers (cleaners of cloth) had been donated by a wealthy priestess called Eumachia. This guild may have been the largest business group in the town and was prominent in local politics. No fewer than 24 electoral notices for AD 79 mention a fuller.

6 Polling station, situated at the end of the Via dell' Abbondanza. Voting in the municipal elections took place here.

7 **The municipal offices** were occupied by the duoviri, the aediles and the decurions, or council, with their staff of clerks and officials. In front of the offices was a colonnade, shown in the picture. (Local government is discussed in Stage 11.)

8 The basilica was not only the courthouse but also a financial centre for businessmen.

9 **Temple of Apollo**, where Apollo and Diana were worshipped. The **cella** was raised on a high podium in the central courtyard, with an altar at the foot of the steps and a sundial on a pedestal at one side. The statue of Apollo (a copy) originally held a bow.

10 On the outside wall of this temple under the portico, there was a recess which contained the **weights and measures table**. Cut into the stone slab was a series of cavities of different sizes in which purchasers could measure the grain or foodstuffs they had bought to ensure that they had been sold the correct quantity. The cavities had holes in the bottom to allow foodstuffs to be collected easily.

p. 52 Detail of carving on lararium from Caecilius' house showing a scene during the earthquake of AD 62. The Temple of Jupiter has an altar in front of it and equestrian statues on either side. The artist has shown only four of the six columns which formed the colonnade at the front of the temple. The scene may commemorate the survival of the family in the earthquake.

Suggested activities

1 *Worksheet Masters* 4.4 and 4.6 are straightforward and focus on the forum.
2 Construct a frieze of the forum as a pedestrian precinct surrounded by colonnades and buildings. Different groups could be allocated different areas and use slides, information from later Stages, and further research to complete the task over a period of time.
3 Exercises in historical empathy (e.g. written account, recording on tape or video, dramatic presentation) could develop the characters, e.g. Clemens bargaining for food in the forum, or Caecilius negotiating a business deal in the Clothworkers' Guildhall.
4 Photocopy this ground plan of the forum and ask students to number the buildings on the plan.

Ground plan of forum

1 Temple of Jupiter
2 Market
3 Temple of the Lares of Pompeii
4 Temple of the Emperors
5 Eumachia's Clothworkers' Guildhall
6 Polling station
7 Municipal offices
8 Basilica
9 Temple of Apollo
10 Table of weights and measures

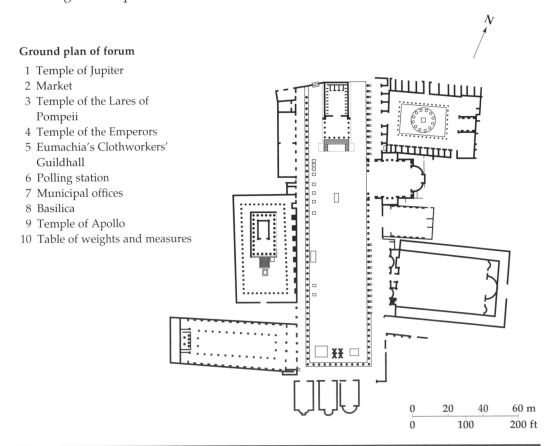

STAGE 5 in theātrō

Cultural background	Story line	Main language features	Focus of exercises
The theatre: actors and performances; pantomime, comedy.	Play attended by all Caecilius' household except Grumio. Poppaea, a slave-girl, has trouble persuading her master, Lucrio, to go to the theatre so that she can meet Grumio.	• Nominative plural. • 3rd person plural present.	1 Agreement of verb with nominative plural. 2 Agreement of verb with nominative singular and plural. 3 Story for translation.

From this Stage onwards teachers should refer to the general notes on teaching method in the Introduction if no specific guidance is given about the handling of the model sentences or stories.

Opening page (p. 53)

Illustration. Detail of Pompeian wall-painting showing tragic mask. The mask represents Oceanus, hence the unusual colour (*Naples, Archaeological Museum*). Vivid and dramatic wall decoration was fashionable. Whole rooms were painted with brightly coloured spectacular scenes of theatrical fantasy (see also p. 15).

Model sentences (pp. 54–7)

New language feature. Plural of nouns and verbs. In this Stage the nominative plural only of nouns is introduced, with the 3rd person plural of the present tense. (The accusative plural is introduced in Stage 8.)

New vocabulary. puella, puer, in theātrō, spectātor, āctor, in scaenā, fēmina, iuvenis, plaudit.

Illustrations. The street scenes depict in simplified form the Via dell' Abbondanza east of the intersection with the Via di Stabia. The theatre is about 180 metres away.

The theatre shown in the drawing at the top of p. 56 is the large open-air one with 5,000 seats shown in the photograph on p. 65. This theatre has an elaborate permanent stone set with statues framed by two tiers of columns. Traces remain of a slot along the front of the stage from which a stage curtain could be raised. The other drawings depict an audience seated in the smaller, roofed theatre shown in the photograph on p. 64. The stage of this theatre has a plain back wall and could have accommodated painted scenery.

The drawing on p. 56 depicts the canvas awning suspended from wooden poles set in sockets round the top of the walls, and stretched across the audience by ropes. The effect of the light filtering through awnings into the auditorium is described by Lucretius (*De rerum natura* IV.75–83).

āctōrēs (p. 58)

Story. This passage describes the effect of the arrival in Pompeii of two well-known actors, Actius and Sorex.

First reading. Guide the class through the story carefully, because there are many new words and phrases. Comparison with modern pop stars will help the class to capture the mood of the passage. A bronze bust of Sorex is shown on p. 64, and a graffito referring to Actius is quoted on p. 65.

Students will enjoy speculating on the reason why Grumio stays behind in the house (line 13), before they find out in the next story.

Consolidation. Re-reading in different ways (see pp. 15–16 of this Guide) is important in helping students to absorb the plural forms and the vocabulary.

Illustrations

p. 58 The two actors shown represent a man (left) and woman from comedy. The statues were originally brightly coloured and stood in the garden of a house near the two theatres at Pompeii (*Naples, Archaeological Museum*).

p. 60 The tragic actor from a Pompeian wall-painting is reflecting on the character he will act (*Naples, Archaeological Museum*).

About the language 1 (pp. 59–60)

New language feature. Plurals. The change from singular to plural is presented in the context of the whole sentence.

Discussion. Elicit the following points:
1 Sentences referring to more than one person or thing are plural.
2 They use a different form of words.
3 Both noun and verb show the difference between singular and plural. Let students see that the same thing occurs in English, e.g. get them to pluralise 'the dog barks' and ask them how many words change.

For the moment concentrate on the verb endings in paragraph 3. Detailed consideration of noun endings is made in 'About the language 2' (p. 62).

The irregularity of **esse** (p. 60, paragraph 4) may cause problems. Compare with English *am, is, are* and forms in French, etc.

Consolidation. Refer the class back to **āctōrēs** and ask them to pick out singular and plural verb forms.

Poppaea (p. 61)

Play. A new character, Poppaea the slave-girl, has difficulty persuading her aged master, Lucrio, to go to the theatre so that she can receive a visit from her boyfriend, Grumio.

First reading. Prepare for a dramatised reading by questioning students about the atmosphere in Pompeii and the attitudes of the characters. The appearance of Grumio makes a satisfying climax and provides the answer to students' speculations.

Consolidation. The dramatised reading requires four characters (narrator, Poppaea, Lucrio, **amīcus**/Grumio), and groups (or the whole class) for **agricolae** and **puerī**.

Discussion of the background information on the comedies of Plautus (pp. 66–7) may be useful in pointing up the characters. The play *Poppaea* can be seen as a simplified illustration of some features of Roman comedy, including the use of stock characters (old man, pretty slave-girl and wily slave) and the elements of intrigue and trickery.

About the language 2 (p. 62)

New language feature. Nominative plural, with 3rd person plural.

Discussion. The focus is mainly on nouns (paragraphs 1–4). As students gain confidence, some examples of other nouns from previous stories could be listed on the board, e.g. **agricolae**, **nautae**, **puerī**, **āctōrēs**, **iuvenēs**, as long as they are seen initially in the context of a complete sentence.

Then move on to paragraph 5 and revise the **-t** and **-nt** inflections of the verb. As with the nouns, further examples from the stories can be highlighted, e.g. **labōrant**, **intrant**, **currunt**, **ambulant**, **contendunt**.

Do not at this stage introduce the complication of the variation between conjugations. This is explained in 'Language information', pp. 182–5.

Consolidation. Further practice examples could be drawn from the *Independent Learning Manual* Stage 5. *Worksheet Master* 5.2 is a listening exercise based on the model sentences.

Practising the language (p. 63)

Exercise 1. Agreement of verb with nominative plural.
Exercise 2. Agreement of verb with nominative singular and plural.
**Exercise 3.* Story. The Pompeians are in the theatre watching a play, which they desert for a performance by a tight-rope walker. The story is based on an incident described in Terence's *Hecyra* Prologue 4.

Cultural background material (pp. 64–7)

Content. The material explains the part played by the theatre in Pompeian life and describes the theatres in Pompeii and the plays put on in them.

The theatre was an established feature of life in the 2nd and 1st centuries BC, when the comedies of Plautus and Terence and some of the old Roman tragedies were regularly performed. Under the Empire, most towns had a theatre. Performances were most frequently pantomime, vulgar farces and one-act plays, with an occasional Plautine comedy.

Discussion. Both text and illustrations are best introduced at the point where they relate to the linguistic material, e.g. 'The theatre at Pompeii' with the model sentences on p. 56, and 'The comedies of Plautus' with **Poppaea** on p. 61.

Illustrations

p. 64 Bronze head of Sorex found in Temple of Isis in Pompeii (*Naples, Archaeological Museum*).

p. 65 The musician playing a form of tambourine is part of a group. Other musicians play double pipes (shown in illustrations on pp. 67, 68) and tiny cymbals. This Pompeian mosaic has exceptionally fine **tesserae** (small mosaic pieces) and is signed by Dioscorides of Samos (*Naples, Archaeological Museum*).

p. 66 A popular type of terracotta mask, unlikely to have been worn in action despite the holes for fastening, but used as an ornament (*Cologne, Römisch-Germanisches Museum*).

p. 67 The pictures represent a standardised comic plot.
(1) Marble relief of scene from comedy (*Naples, Archaeological Museum*).
(2) Detail from mosaic of theatrical masks. Note the double pipe behind the mask (*Rome, Capitoline Museums*).
(3) The slave has been with his master at a party as can be seen from the wreath he is wearing. Terracotta statuette (*British Museum*).
(4) Most comedies have a recognition scene to bring about their dénouement. Fragment of mosaic (*Naples, Archaeological Museum*).

p. 68 Detail from Pompeian wall-painting. Satyr dancing on a **thyrsus**, the wand carried by followers of Dionysus (*Naples, Archaeological Museum*).

Suggested activities

1 Dramatic reading or performance of a scene from a Roman comedy in translation, such as *Worksheet Master* 5.6.
2 Write a short play to fit the sequence of illustrations on p. 67.
3 Using the illustrations in this Stage, draw and colour a theatrical mask or make one. *Worksheet Master* 5.7 provides templates of two masks.

STAGE 6 Fēlīx

Cultural background	Story line	Main language features	Focus of exercises
Slaves and freedmen.	After witnessing a fight in the forum, Clemens bumps into one of Caecilius' freedmen, Felix, and takes him home. Caecilius and Metella invite him for dinner and recall the incident which earned Felix his freedom.	• Imperfect and perfect (**v**-stems) in 3rd person singular and plural. • **erat** and **erant**.	1 Story with comprehension questions. 2 Agreement of nominative singular and plural with verb.

Opening page (p. 69)

Illustration. Relief probably showing manumission ceremony. The magistrate stands holding the rod with which he has freed two former slaves. The conical felt cap (**pilleus**) which they are wearing is a mark of their new status as freedmen. The standing freedman appears to be shaking hands with his master, whose figure has been lost from the right-hand side of the relief; the other one is kneeling to him in gratitude (*Morlanwelz, Belgium, Musée royale de Mariemont*).

Model sentences (pp. 70–1)

New language feature. Introduction of two past tenses, perfect and imperfect, in the 3rd person. In this Stage, the perfect tense has only the form in **v**, e.g. **clāmāvit**. The imperfects **erat** and **erant** are also introduced.

New vocabulary. timēbat, superāvit, pulsāvit (*punched*).

First reading. Students may ask about the new endings. There is no signal in the text to indicate the change to past time, so you need to give an explicit lead, e.g.:
Sentence 1. What were the slaves doing?

In English, as in Latin, it is characteristic for the imperfect to be used to describe a situation, and the perfect to represent a momentary happening. The pairs of sentences highlight the contrast between the situation and the action which interrupts it, e.g. 'The slaves *were walking* when the dog *barked*.' See the *Independent Learning Manual* Stage 6 for a cartoon showing the difference between the present and two past tenses.

Initially, it is sufficient for students to see the difference in terms of their English translation. It is helpful to use forms like *were walking* and *was annoying* consistently for the imperfect, wherever possible, moving gradually towards a more flexible approach in later Stages as students gain confidence in recognising the forms. It may help to have some of the sentences and their translations written on the board or OHP in two columns, one for each tense.

Consolidation. Encourage students to create some simple rules of their own for recognising and translating the tenses. They will be more likely to remember and use principles which they have established for themselves. They will probably work out that the endings **-bat** and **-bant** correspond to the English forms *was …ing* and *were …ing* and that **v** denotes the shorter form of the past tense, e.g. *walked*, *shouted*.

pugna (p. 72)

Story. Clemens is strolling in the forum observing the activities around him when a fight breaks out between a farmer and a Greek merchant.

First reading. This passage contains descriptions of situations interrupted by momentary actions. You can reinforce the difference between the perfect and the imperfect by using such questions as:

Where was Clemens walking?
Why did Clemens hurry when he heard the noise?
What did the farmer do to the Greek?
What were the Pompeians doing?
Which Latin word tells you the fight went on for some time?
Why did the Pompeians support the farmer?

quod and **postquam** occur here for the first time and sentences become longer. It is helpful if students listen to and then repeat these sentences in Latin, stressing the pauses at the comma boundaries and getting the intonation right. **quod** and **postquam** are relatively colourless words and it takes time for students to master them.

Consolidation. When the class has understood the story, ask students to produce translations individually, or in pairs or groups, and then compare and discuss the alternatives. This provides another opportunity to highlight the two tenses. The *Independent Learning Manual* Stage 6 has an exercise based on this story which practises the tenses.

Fēlīx (p. 72)

Story. Clemens meets Felix in a bar and takes him home, where he is welcomed by Caecilius and Metella, and moved by seeing Quintus.

First reading. Use the question and answer technique. Possible questions are to be found on p. 14 of this Guide.

An emotional moment occurs in line 9 (**paene lacrimābat; sed rīdēbat.**). Encourage the class to recognise the feelings and speculate on the reasons for them. The explanation emerges in the next story. If students find **lacrimābat** difficult because the nominative is omitted, ask them what the meaning of **lībertus … lacrimābat** would be and then the meaning without the noun.

Similarly, students might reflect on Grumio's happiness in line 12. Had Felix been a good friend of Grumio's when he was a member of Caecilius' household?

Consolidation. The *Independent Learning Manual* Stage 6 contains consolidation exercises for both stories.

Fēlīx et fūr (p. 73)

Story. Felix and Caecilius explain to Quintus how Felix earned his freedom.

First reading. At the end of the story, remind students of the emotion shown by Felix in line 9 of the previous story, so that they can reflect on the relationships revealed by his feelings.

Consolidation. If this story is acted, the content of Caecilius' second speech can be mimed. You will need four actors: Caecilius, Quintus, Felix and the thief. Discussion about character and situation provides the stimulus to study the information about slaves and freedmen (pp. 78–81). This is a good story to represent as a cartoon, using sentences from the story as captions.

About the language (pp. 74–5)

New language features. Imperfect and perfect tenses (**v**- stems) in 3rd person singular and plural; **erat** and **erant**.

Gather together the rules which students have evolved with you so far, and introduce the language note as a development of their own ideas. Read paragraphs 1–4.

Consolidation. Reinforce these paragraphs immediately with oral translation of further examples, written on a board or OHP. Use only complete sentences, and present one contrast at a time, e.g.:

1 Caecilius in tablīnō labōrābat. servī cibum in forō quaerēbant.
   Metella in ātriō sedēbat. Caecilius et Quīntus in viā ambulābant.
   spectātōrēs erant in theātrō. āctor erat in scaenā.
   imperfect singular with *imperfect plural*
2 īnfāns in cubiculō dormiēbat. fūr per iānuam intrāvit.
   mercātor pecūniam nōn reddēbat. Caecilius mercātōrem ad basilicam
   vocāvit.
   imperfect singular with *perfect singular*
3 cīvēs ad theātrum contendēbant. nūntiī fābulam nūntiāvērunt.
   imperfect plural with *perfect plural*

Now read paragraphs 5 and 6, which introduce the ideas of continuous and momentary or completed action. Test students' grasp of these distinctions by asking them about the contrasting verbs in the examples in 2 and 3 above.

Illustration. Bar at Herculaneum. The woodwork survives remarkably well. Visible are the railing of a mezzanine floor, a rack containing eight amphorae suspended from the wall, and a large storage jar buried in the ground, left.

Practising the language (pp. 76–7)

**Exercise 1.* Story with comprehension questions. Thieves intending to rob a miser of his money are thwarted by his faithful slave, a snake. The level of difficulty of the story is the same as in the main reading passages, and the new language features are included. You may need to help students with their first reading, and judge when they are ready to tackle the comprehension questions. The answers and mark scheme are as follows:

		Marks
1	Two thieves.	1
2	The merchant was an old man and a miser. He had a lot of money.	3
3	The thieves looked round the atrium.	1
4	The thief thought the merchant did not have a slave.	1
5	**ferōciter pugnāvit**.	2
	It was two against one/The merchant was an old man.	1
6	A faithful slave.	1
	The thief thought the merchant did not have a faithful slave because he was a miser.	2
7	A bedroom.	1
	A huge snake lying on the money.	2
8	The thieves were afraid of the snake.	1
9	A very good slave.	1
	The snake never slept. It always looked after his money.	2
10	The merchant was counting some money/doing his accounts *or similar*.	1
	TOTAL	20

Exercise 2. Agreement of nominative singular and plural with verb and additional practice in translating imperfect and perfect.

Additional exercises on the tenses are to be found in *Worksheet Master* 6.3 and in the *Independent Learning Manual* Stage 6.

If students need further practice with **postquam** and **quod**, use *Worksheet Master* 6.2.

Illustration. Cobra, detail from wall-painting found in Pompeii (*Naples, Archaeological Museum*).

Cultural background material (pp. 78–81)

Content. The institution of slavery; the work and treatment of slaves; **manūmissiō**; freedmen. Since there is no direct parallel in present-day western society, and slavery in other societies had a different rationale, slavery needs to be explained in terms of actual Roman practice. This is complex because the condition and role of Roman slaves varied at different times and places, and with different masters, ranging from a relationship of respect and mutual confidence to resentment and extreme brutality.

Discussion. It is useful to introduce the material in the context of the stories, **Fēlīx** (p. 72) and **Fēlīx et fūr** (p. 73), where it illuminates character and relationships. This is a good opportunity to review earlier Stages, where slaves have already featured prominently. Discussion can start from the familiar situation, e.g.:

What relationship does there seem to be between Caecilius and his slaves?
What sort of jobs did the slaves in his household perform?
What aspects of Grumio's life as a slave might he dislike? What compensations might he find in it?
What might Felix say to Grumio about his life as a freedman?

It can then develop towards a wider view and greater realism, e.g.:

What other work was done by slaves in Pompeii?
What difficulties would face a young person brought from a distant country into slavery in Roman society?

The topic is further explored later in the course.

Further information. The cost of slaves in the 1st century AD ranged from approximately 800 to 8,000 sesterces, but especially attractive or gifted slaves would be priced higher. The highest recorded price was 700,000 sesterces paid for the grammarian Lutatius Daphnis, who was then immediately freed. Compare this with other prices of the time, e.g.:

1,200 sesterces (300 denarii) – legionary's annual pay.
10,000 sesterces – highest permitted fee for lawyer.
1,000,000 sesterces – property qualification for senator.

Illustrations

p. 78 Detail from lid of sarcophagus of AD 160–70 representing battle between Romans and Gauls (*Rome, Capitoline Museums*).

p. 79 • Slave serving drinks, from carving on 3rd-century tomb from Neumagen. He stands by a table on which are an amphora and a wine-strainer (*Trier, Rheinisches Landesmuseum*).

• Nurse with baby in cradle from 3rd-century memorial (*Cologne, Römisch-Germanisches Museum*).

• Top surface of lamp showing eight men carrying barrel slung from two shoulder poles (*British Museum*).

• Mosaic head, perhaps of gladiator, from Baths of Caracalla (*Rome, Museo Nazionale Romano*).

p. 80 Overseer beating man with cane, from Mosaic of the Great Hunt, Piazza Armerina, Sicily.

p. 81 Peristyle, House of the Vettii, Pompeii. Reveals the wealth acquired by many freedmen.

p. 82 Cupids drawn by deer in chariot race, in triclinium of House of the Vettii, Pompeii.

Suggested activities

1 You are Syphax composing an advertisement for a slave. Give details of name, age, nationality, previous history, skills and price.

2 *Worksheet Master* 6.5 is a game based on the imaginary lives of two slaves.

Vocabulary checklist (p. 82)

rēs is here translated as *thing* for the sake of simplicity, but discuss with students the range of meanings the word acquires in different contexts. So far students have met:

rem probat   *he proves the case* (p. 44, lines 24–5, 30).

rem nārrāvit   *he told the story* (p. 73, line 3).

rem audīvit   *he heard the story* (p. 73, line 20).

To reinforce the point that words may have more than one possible translation, refer students to p. 190, paragraph 7.

STAGE 7 cēna

Cultural background	Story line	Main language features	Focus of exercises
Roman beliefs about life after death.	At Caecilius' dinner party, Felix tells a story about a werewolf. A missing guest is found dead. Metella comforts Melissa when she is upset by criticism from Grumio and Clemens.	• Sentence pattern: ACCUSATIVE + VERB (i.e. nominative omitted). • Perfect tense (other than forms in **v**).	1 Selection of verbal phrase to match nominative. 2 Selection of nominative or accusative singular; nominative singular or plural.

Opening page (p. 83)

Illustration. Mosaic of a skeleton butler, holding a wine jug in each hand, found in a triclinium in Pompeii (*Naples, Archaeological Museum*). Romans often introduced images of death to their dining-rooms as a reminder of the transience of life and the need to enjoy its pleasures while they could.

Model sentences (pp. 84–5)

New language features. Sentence structure ACCUSATIVE + VERB (i.e. nominative omitted). Perfect tenses, with forms in **s**, **ss**, **x** and **u**.

New vocabulary. pōculum, īnspexit, hausit, valē.

First reading. Establish the meaning with comprehension questions before asking for the pair of sentences to be translated together, e.g.:
  Sentence 2. What was Caecilius doing? What did *he* do next?

fābula mīrābilis (p. 86)

Story. Felix entertains Caecilius' dinner guests with a story about a centurion who turns out to be a werewolf. The story is based on Petronius, *Satyrica* 62.

First reading. This is the first of three stories touching on the supernatural. Heighten the atmosphere by making the reading in Latin as dramatic as possible, and by choosing tantalising points to break off and explore the meaning, e.g.:
  Decēns nōn adest (line 4).
  … subitō centuriōnem cōnspexit (line 10).
  ingēns lupus subitō appāruit (line 12).

Illustration. The atmospheric background for the werewolf is derived from a wall-painting found in the Temple of Isis in Pompeii (*Naples, Archaeological Museum*).

About the language 1 (p. 87)

New language feature. Sentence structure ACCUSATIVE + VERB (i.e. nominative omitted).

Discussion. When students translate the examples in paragraph 4, they may need help with example **d**. If they translate **Grumiōnem salūtāvērunt** as *Grumio greeted them*, compare the sentence with **lībertī Grumiōnem salūtāvērunt**. If necessary, refer them back to the sentences in paragraph 2. When students produce the correct translation, respond, 'Yes, they greeted Grumio, but where is the word for *they*? How can you tell the sentence means *"they* greeted Grumio"?' Analysis in terms of accusative, verb and unexpressed nominative will not help most students.

Consolidation. In designing further examples, use the device of paired sentences with the subject made explicit in the first sentence. *Worksheet Master* 7.3 provides useful practice.

Illustration. Detail from mosaic representing unswept floor of dining-room (*Rome, Vatican Museums*). This design, based on a Hellenistic original, was popular in the ancient world.

Decēns (p. 88)

Play. Decens has failed to arrive for the dinner party. His slaves report his encounter with a ghostly gladiator, and Clemens' discovery of his body in the arena.

First reading. Some students find the story of the gladiator confusing, so make sure that they are clear about the events reported by the slaves.

Be prepared for heated discussion about the supernatural. Sceptics could be invited to find a rational reason for Decens' death. Perhaps his slaves murdered him?

Consolidation. The play could be acted by two sets of students: one reading the parts of Caecilius, Clemens and the two slaves; and the other taking the parts of Decens and the gladiator in the speeches of the slaves.

Exercises could be developed on several of the language features in this story, e.g. the personal endings of the present tense and easily forgotten or confused words (**cōnspexit, valdē, tamen, petīvit, rem intellegō, ōlim**).

**post cēnam (p. 89)

Story. The guests depart nervously, scattering noisily when alarmed by a cat. Caecilius sleeps unperturbed.

First reading. The content of this story does not bear repetition. It is appropriate sometimes to let one reading suffice, in order to demonstrate to students their growing competence and your confidence in them.

Illustrations
- Detail of stone mask decorating the courtyard of House of Neptune and Amphitrite in Herculaneum, photographed in a thunderstorm.
- Mosaic of cat with small bird, perhaps a quail. A popular theme. This version is from a villa near Rome; a similar one was found in the House of the Faun, Pompeii. (*Rome, Museo Nazionale Romano*)

About the language 2 (p. 90)

New language feature. Further forms of the perfect.

Discussion
Paragraph 1. Students should recognise the perfect form in **v**, which has already been explained (p. 74). If necessary, list more examples from recent stories, reading the sentences aloud and writing up the verbs in the format they are about to meet in paragraph 2, e.g.:

	PRESENT	PERFECT	
		singular	*plural*
omnēs ad ātrium festīnāvērunt.	festīnat	festīnāvit	festīnāvērunt
gladiātor clāmāvit.	clāmat	clāmāvit	clāmāvērunt

Paragraph 2. After discussing the new forms, guide students to supply further examples from the model sentences or the stories they have read and add them to the list, e.g.:

Caecilius et hospitēs plausērunt.	plaudit	plausit	plausērunt
dominus gladiātōrem cōnspexit.	cōnspicit	cōnspexit	cōnspexērunt

Note. Students may not have met or remembered the present tense of some of the new perfect forms.

Students are often adept at composing mnemonics. Ask them to invent mnemonics for the 'key' letters of the perfect, i.e. v x u s, and then vote for the best one, which everyone learns.

Paragraph 3. Leave this until the next lesson and then read with students the explanation about the listing of verbs on p. 189, paragraphs 4 and 5. Ask them to do the examples in paragraph 6 (p. 190). They may need help with the last example, **accēpit**, which does not occur in its perfect or present forms until Stages 9 and 10 respectively.

Metella et Melissa (p. 91)

Story. Metella finds Melissa in tears because Grumio and Clemens have been angry with her. She comforts the slave-girl by praising her work.

First reading. Contrast Metella's sympathetic treatment of Melissa with her earlier attitude (p. 31) and discuss the reasons for the change.

The use of **heri** and **hodiē** will help students with the frequent changes of time. Where these indicators are lacking, you may need to use leading comprehension questions, e.g.:

What was Metella doing?

What is the question she asks Grumio?

Consolidation. Written translation of part of this story is a useful way of checking that students have learned to recognise the different tenses and personal endings. The story is also suitable for acting.

Practising the language (p. 92)

Exercise 1. Selection of a phrase containing a verb in the perfect tense, to match a singular or plural nominative. Remind students of the endings **-t** and **-nt**. The last three examples are more difficult.

Exercise 2. Selection of nouns in the nominative or accusative singular and the nominative singular or plural. Point out to students that there are two points being practised here and help them with a couple of examples if necessary.

Other suitable exercises are to be found in the *Independent Learning Manual* Stage 7 and in *Worksheet Master* 7.5.

Cultural background material (pp. 93–5)

Content. Following the stories about the supernatural, this section gives a general picture of Roman beliefs about life after death and funerary practices.

Discussion. Take care to discover beforehand if any student may, because of personal circumstances, find death a painful topic. If handled sensitively, discussion can be helpful on a number of levels. Questions for discussion and study include:

1 Why did most people in the ancient world die at a comparatively young age by modern western standards?

2 What memorials and customs kept the memory of the dead alive in Roman times? How different are these today?

3 Why may the excavation of tombs be helpful to archaeologists seeking to reconstruct the daily life of the time?

4 What modern beliefs are there about life after death?

A possible group activity is to gather together Roman beliefs about life after death by re-reading this section and studying the illustrations on pp. 93–6. Students could also examine the tomb inscriptions in the *Independent Learning Manual* Stage 7.

Illustrations

p. 93 • Street of Tombs looking towards Herculaneum Gate, Pompeii. Note the variety of design. Tombs were usually situated by the side of important roads leading out of the town but were sometimes placed on rural estates.

• Interior of a tomb in the Street of Tombs, with recesses for ashes. It probably belonged to Aulus Umbricius Scaurus, one of the most successful Pompeian manufacturers of **garum** (fish sauce), for which Pompeii was famous.

p. 94 • Cylindrical lead canister buried in stone-lined pit (*Caerleon, Roman Legionary Museum*). The stone is pierced by a feeding pipe (originally considerably longer) through which wine, milk or honey could be poured.

• The Blue Vase. Like the Portland Vase, this was made by the cameo technique. A layer of white glass was spread over the blue glass and then carved to form the design of cupids celebrating while harvesting grapes (*Naples, Archaeological Museum*).

• Amphorae from the cemetery at Isola Sacra, Ostia.

p. 95 • This dining-room, now poorly preserved, is shown in a 19th-century wood engraving. It has three masonry couches grouped round a circular table.

• Head of Epicurus from Villa of the Papyri at Herculaneum (*Naples, Archaeological Museum*). This villa belonged to a wealthy Roman with a large library of Epicurean philosophical works, mostly in Greek. The J. Paul Getty Museum at Malibu, California, is housed in a reconstruction of this villa.

p. 96 Relief of wrong-doers punished in the underworld, from a sarcophagus (*Rome, Vatican Museums*).

Suggested activities

Worksheet Master 7.7, exercise on beliefs about life after death. See also the *Independent Learning Manual* Stage 7.

STAGE 8 gladiātōrēs

Cultural background	Story line	Main language features	Focus of exercises
The amphi-theatre and gladiatorial shows.	A senator called Regulus gives a gladiatorial show at Pompeii which ends in a riot. The story of Androcles and the lion.	• Accusative plural. • Superlative.	1 1st and 2nd person singular of present; accusative plural. 2 1st, 2nd and 3rd person singular of present.

Opening page (p. 97)

Illustration. Top surface of a Roman clay lamp. This shows two fighters, bare chested, each armed with helmet, pair of greaves, protection on sword arm, straight sword and oblong shield. One contestant has dropped his shield (*Trier, Rheinisches Landesmuseum*).

Gladiators were a popular theme on lamps. The names of about 20 types of gladiator are known but few can be identified from the evidence of representations like this.

Model sentences (pp. 98–9)

New language feature. The accusative plural is now introduced within the basic sentence.

New vocabulary. spectāculum, nūntiābant, clausae, murmillōnēs, saepe, victōrēs.

gladiātōrēs (p. 100)

Story. Regulus, a Roman senator who lives near Nuceria, puts on a gladiatorial show in the amphitheatre at Pompeii since the Nucerians do not have an amphitheatre of their own. The Pompeians are angered by the congestion caused by the influx of Nucerians, but initially calm prevails in the amphitheatre.

First reading. This story needs careful planning because it presents a number of challenges. It contains little action, but is important in setting the scene and creating the atmosphere for later stories in this Stage. There are some long sentences containing subordinate clauses introduced by **quod**, **postquam** and **ubi**. Two contrasting strategies are:
1 To work on the material about gladiatorial shows (pp. 107–10) before reading this story, to enable students to approach with more confidence the situations described in the Latin.

2 To give nothing away in advance, heightening students' awareness of impending trouble when reading the story, e.g.:

... erant inimīcī (line 2)

saepe erant turbulentī (line 4)

... Nūcerīnī viās complēbant (lines 7–8)

omnēs vehementer clāmābant (line 15).

Longer sentences. These usually follow an order which is familiar in English, but sometimes the subordinate clause is embedded in the main clause, e.g.:

Nūcerīnī, quod amphitheātrum nōn habēbant, saepe ad amphitheātrum Pompēiānum veniēbant (lines 3–4).

Pompēiānī, postquam nūntiōs audīvērunt, ad amphitheātrum quam celerrimē contendērunt (lines 13–14).

To give students extra help here, you could:

1 Read the Latin sentences aloud with emphasis and appropriate pauses to demarcate the clauses.

2 After the first reading, break the complex sentence down into simple sentences for students to translate, e.g.:

Nūcerīnī amphitheātrum nōn habēbant. Nūcerīnī saepe ad amphitheātrum Pompēiānum veniēbant.

and then knit it together again with the conjunction.

Illustration. Amphitheatre at Pompeii, built in first half of 1st century BC, shown from the north. One of the external staircases gives access to seats at the top and the retaining wall encircles the embankment of earth created to support the seats by excavating the centre of the arena.

in arēnā (p. 101)

Story. A contest between a pair of **rētiāriī**, supported by the Nucerians, and a pair of **murmillōnēs**, the Pompeians' favourites, is won by the retiarii. The retiarii exploit their superior mobility, the murmillones their superior equipment.

First reading. This is a difficult story. Students often have a problem with the terms retiarius and murmillo and the whole story hinges on the difference between the two and their supporters. Notes, stick figures and a diagram of the fight on the board or OHP can help here. Use comprehension questions to draw students' attention to the tactical element, e.g.:

Why did the retiarii at first avoid a fight?

Were the Pompeians right to say that the retiarii were **ignāvī**?

Why did the first murmillo attack the two retiarii on his own?

Was this what the retiarii had been hoping for?

Consolidation. Change the focus of discussion to the reaction of the spectators, e.g.:

Why did the Pompeians ask for mercy for the murmillones?

What made the Nucerians demand their death?

Why do you think Regulus sided with the Nucerians?

If you are short of time there is a useful cartoon version of this story in the *Independent Learning Manual* Stage 8.

Illustration. Retiarius, armed with trident (in origin a fishing-spear) and net, wearing a distinctive shoulder-guard on right shoulder. Relief from Chester (*Saffron Walden Museum*).

About the language 1 (p. 102)

New language feature. Accusative plural.

Discussion. You may wish to remind students of their first introduction to the accusative and the term *case* (p. 21), and the first table of accusatives (p. 32).

After they have translated the examples in paragraph 4, ask them to indicate which word is the accusative and give its number, e.g.:

The farmer praised the gladiator (*accusative singular*).

The farmer praised the gladiators (*accusative plural*).

Consolidation. Students could:

1 Pick out examples of the accusative plural in stories they have already read.

2 Supply the Latin for words in English sentences by using the table in the text, e.g.:

Quintus greets *the girls*. Caecilius welcomes *the merchants*.

Extend this by mixing both singular and plural forms of the accusative.

3 Do further exercises on cases: *Worksheet Master* 8.4 and *Independent Learning Manual* Stage 8.

vēnātiō (p. 103)

Story. The beast-fight at Regulus' games. The uncharacteristic behaviour of the lions on this occasion fuels the growing animosity between Pompeians and Nucerians, and a riot occurs.

First reading. Students should first read the information about beast-fights (p. 110). They should explore the complete story before attempting the comprehension questions. Give help, if necessary, with the complex sentences (see note on **gladiātōrēs** on pp. 60–1 of the Guide). The answers and mark scheme are as follows. Give credit for any sensible answer.

		Marks
1	The trumpet sounded again. Suddenly a lot of deer entered the arena.	2
2	They felt frightened.	1
	The dogs (chased and) killed them.	2
3	They were hungry, and easily overcame the dogs.	2
4	The Nucerians were very happy, the Pompeians were dissatisfied.	2
5	They wanted to see the lions/They thought Regulus was holding the lions back.	1
6	Immediately three lions rushed in through the gate.	2
7	The lions would attack the beast-fighters.	2
	The lions lay down in the arena and fell asleep.	1
8	Regulus was putting on a ridiculous show. They chased Regulus and the Nucerians from the amphitheatre.	2
9	The Pompeians (drew their swords and) killed many Nucerians.	1
10	**ecce** emphasises the drama/seriousness of the riot/points up the irony of bloodshed in the streets rather than in the amphitheatre.	2
	TOTAL	20

Consolidation. *Worksheet Master* 8.2 contains examples of complex sentences based on some of the incidents in this story.

In further discussion of the story, the information about the riot (p. 111) will be useful.

**pāstor et leō (p. 104)

Story. The story of Androcles and the lion is based on Aulus Gellius, V.14.30.

First reading. This is a revision piece containing examples of most of the noun and verb endings introduced so far, in particular the 1st and 2nd person of the present.

Consolidation. Students could draw a cartoon version of the story, selecting suitable sentences as captions. There is an exercise based on this story in *Worksheet Master* 8.3.

Illustration. Mosaic of seemingly unhappy lion (*Tunis, Bardo Museum*).

About the language 2 (p. 105)

New language feature. Superlative.

Discussion. Remind students that this note sums up a linguistic feature which has occurred several times earlier in the Course.

Consolidation. Revisit in context regular superlatives which students have already met, e.g.:

Grumiō est laetissimus (p. 20).

Pugnāx erat gladiātor nōtissimus (p. 88).

canēs erant fortissimī, sed lupī facile canēs superāvērunt (p. 103).

Nūcerīnī erant laetissimī (p. 103).

tum Pompēiānī erant īrātissimī (p. 103).

If students ask about **optimus**, which occurs very frequently, confirm that it is a superlative, but an irregular one. Compare English by asking the class if the superlative of 'good' is 'goodest'. Postpone further discussion until Book II where irregular comparatives and superlatives are presented.

There is an exercise on superlatives in the *Independent Learning Manual* Stage 8.

Illustration. Wall-painting from tomb of C. Vestorius Priscus who died aged 22, three or four years before the destruction of the city (*Pompeii, in situ*).

Practising the language (p. 106)

Exercise 1. Revision of 1st and 2nd person singular of present; further practice with accusative plural.

Exercise 2. Revision of the 1st, 2nd and 3rd person singular of present (introduced in Stage 4).

Illustration. Two arena musicians playing curved horn and organ. The emotions of the spectators were heightened, as in a modern circus, by the musical accompaniment. Straight trumpets were also played (*Germany, 3rd-century Roman villa at Nennig*).

Cultural background material (pp. 107–11)

Content. Description of the amphitheatre and the kind of gladiatorial fights and beast hunts that took place in it; a translation of the account of the riot in the amphitheatre at Pompeii (Tacitus, *Annals* XIV.17).

Discussion. The amphitheatre is an emotive subject. The following topics may be helpful:

1 A comparison with modern forms of popular entertainment, including boxing, motor racing, bull-fighting, field sports. Similarities include the element of danger and violence. Differences include the fact that gladiators were normally aiming to kill each other, and that they generally had no choice about participating.

2 The reactions of the spectators, ranging from sadistic enjoyment to analytical appreciation of the performance of highly trained and skilled practitioners.

3 The fascination that violence has for people.

Further information. The amphitheatre at Pompeii, built in about 80 BC, is the earliest surviving amphitheatre, predating the first permanent arena in Rome by 50 years. It seated 20,000 spectators and measured 130 × 102 metres. Its main features included the tiers of stone benches, the barrier which separated the spectators from the arena, and the impressive exterior arcading and staircases.

Gladiatorial shows usually took place in amphitheatres, occasionally in fora.

Illustrations

p. 107 • Interior of amphitheatre at Pompeii, viewed along long axis.
        • Detail from Pompeian wall-painting showing the riot of AD 59. At the top is the awning. People are fighting in the arena, in the seating and outside (*Naples, Archaeological Museum*).

p. 108 Drawings based on stucco frieze in Pompeian tomb. Audience added by illustrator.

p. 109 • Pompeian statue of Thracian gladiator, possibly used as tavern sign, with a small statuette (to right) of the god Priapus. Thracians were armed with a small shield, either round (as here) or square, and a curved sword.
        • Examples of gladiator armour (*Naples, Archaeological Museum*).

p. 110 • Drawing based on same series of reliefs as p. 108.
        • Fragment of wall-painting, similar to finds at Pompeii, from amphitheatre at Merida, Spain, showing beast-fighter with spear facing lioness (*Merida, National Museum of Roman Art*).

p. 111 • Drawing based on same wall-painting as shown on p. 107.
        • Graffito showing victorious gladiator with palm, the symbol of victory; linked to the riot by writing below:

CAMPANI VICTORIA VNA	Campanians, in your moment
CVM NVCERINIS PERISTIS	of victory you have perished along with the Nucerians (taking **ūnā** closely with **cum**; a less likely interpretation would be *in one victory*)

        Campānī seems to refer to the inhabitants of one of the wards in Pompeii, not to those of the region of Campania.

p. 112 Dead gladiator from 4th-century mosaic of gladiatorial combats, from Torre Nuova. His name, Aureus, is given on the mosaic though not in this detail (*Rome, Borghese Gallery*).

Suggested activities

1 Two gladiators are waiting in the tunnel just before going out into the arena to fight. They have trained together and are personal friends. What might they have said to each other?

2

This pottery fragment in the Jewry Wall Museum, Leicester, is scratched with the graffito **Verecunda [et] ludia Lucius gladiator**, linking the name of an actress with that of a gladiator. What might the actress say to her gladiator to dissuade him from going on fighting in the arena, now that he has been presented with his wooden sword? What reasons might he give for continuing?

3   Additional activities might include: designing posters, creating a diorama (instructions on *Worksheet Master* 8.6), producing a radio programme with taped commentary and discussions, or a newspaper report of a fight. ICT will enable students to produce a more professional piece of work.

Vocabulary checklist (p. 112)

For written tests, use the Latin form given in the list (nominative singular of nouns, 3rd person present of verbs). For oral practice from now on, try using other forms of words in the list (e.g. nominative plural of nouns, perfect tense of verbs), asking students to translate them appropriately.

STAGE 9 thermae

Cultural background	Story line	Main language features	Focus of exercises
The Roman baths.	Quintus celebrates his birthday by visiting the baths. He tries out his new discus with disastrous results. Metella buys Quintus a new toga as a present. A toga thief is caught in the baths.	Dative singular and plural.	1 Selection of verb according to sense. 2 Agreement of verb with a nominative singular or plural. 3 Completion exercise based on **in tabernā**. All exercises practise dative singular and plural.

Opening page (p. 113)

Illustration. Centrepiece of entrance hall, surrounded by two tiers of arches and dramatically lit by skylight above. The marble bust of Apollo incorporated a jet of water that played into the circular basin in front of it (*Suburban Baths, Herculaneum*).

Model sentences (pp. 114–15)

New language feature. The dative case (singular and plural) is introduced within the basic sentence, after the nominative, i.e. NOMINATIVE + DATIVE + ACCUSATIVE + VERB.

New vocabulary. ad thermās, discum novum, ferēbat, statuam, percussit, nāsum frāctum, dōnum, togās, ēlēgit.

Consolidation. Re-read at the start of subsequent lessons the sentences which relate to the coming story.

Illustrations
p. 114 The building in the background to these line drawings combines elements from various baths in Pompeii and Herculaneum.
p. 115 The original of the amphora rack is on p. 75; a very similar lantern appears on p. 176.

in palaestrā (pp. 116–17)

Story. Caecilius takes Quintus to the baths where he meets a famous athlete and, in trying out his new discus, offends him by chipping his statue. The answers and mark scheme are as follows. Give credit for any sensible answer.

		Marks
1	Because he was celebrating his birthday.	1
2	So that Quintus could try out his discus in the palaestra/ show it off to his friends.	2
3	Young men and athletes.	1
4	The Pompeians put up statues to very well-known athletes.	2
5	**ingēns, nōtissimus**. He was huge and very famous.	2
6	He was vain/wanted to make sure people were watching/ had safety in mind/was working out his throw.	2
7	They praised him. The discus flew through the air a long way/It was a huge throw.	2
8	A slave had retrieved the discus and returned it to Milo. He was offering it to the athlete. *Give credit for any two good points.*	2
9	The discus hit a statue and broke its nose.	2
10	Milo was furious; the Pompeians were laughing. No: he was wrong; he should have seen the funny side of the accident/realised how ridiculous his anger was. Yes: Quintus had been careless and damaged a valuable object.	2

TOTAL 20

In discussing students' answers, there are opportunities:

1 To practise the perfect and imperfect tenses in the way suggested on p. 16 of this Guide.

2 To encourage students to explore more deeply the motivation of the characters, e.g.:

> Why did Quintus break the statue? Was he nervous? Careless? Showing off in front of his friends?
> Why did the bystanders laugh at the accident? Why did Quintus? Why did Milo not laugh?

3 To help students appreciate the Roman idea of honour, for oneself and the community, by exploring the attitudes shown to and by Milo, e.g.:

> Do students regard him as arrogant? Would his contemporaries?
> Under what circumstances might the statue have been erected?
> Had he won a deciding event in an athletics match against Nuceria?
> Had he won a victory in Rome, bringing honour to his home town?
> Do modern athletes enjoy the same importance and status?

Illustration

p. 117 Palaestra (*Stabian Baths, Pompeii*). These baths originated before the Roman colony was established in the early 1st century BC, and have a large exercise ground which relates to the days when the city's culture was more Greek than Roman.

About the language (pp. 118–19)

New language feature. Dative singular and plural.

Discussion. This is a long note and teachers may wish to deal with paragraph 5 in a separate lesson. Start by putting this pair of model sentences with their translations on the board or OHP:

multī hospitēs cum Quīntō cēnābant.

Clēmēns hospitibus vīnum offerēbat.

Proceed as for the accusative on p. 30 of this Guide. Then read the language note.

Consolidation. Ask students to pick out sentences containing a dative from stories they have already read, and have the sentences translated in full to remind them of the function of the dative. Do not at this stage expect them to cope with the dative in isolation. See also *Worksheet Master* 9.3 and the *Independent Learning Manual* Stage 9.

in tabernā (p. 120)

Story. Metella goes shopping to buy Quintus a new toga as a birthday present. When her choice proves expensive, Melissa beats down the price.

First reading. Keep a tally on the board or OHP of Marcellus' demands and Melissa's offers.

Consolidation. After the reading is complete, discuss some of the issues which emerge, e.g. Who makes the decision to buy the toga? Why does Melissa do all the bargaining? Where do people bargain like this today?

Exercise 3 on p. 121 consolidates this story. *Worksheet Master* 9.4 is a dramatic dialogue based on the story.

Illustration. This relief of a fabric shop shows two customers (sitting down) attended by a slave, inspecting a piece of cloth. The salesman in the centre and his two assistants may also be slaves.

Practising the language (p. 121)

Exercise 1. Selection of verb for sense. Practice with dative.
Exercise 2. Agreement of verb in the perfect with a nominative singular or plural. Practice with dative.
Exercise 3. Completion exercise based on **in tabernā**. With one exception, **a**, the missing word is in the accusative case.

Language information: revision

In Stage 7 students learnt how verbs were listed in the general vocabulary. Now is a good time to do the same for nouns. The explanation and practice exercise are set out on p. 189, paragraphs 1–3. Further examples could be taken from recent stories and vocabulary checklists.

**in apodytēriō (p. 122)

Play. Two attendants in the apodyterium apprehend a man stealing a toga.

First reading. This story is harder than it looks because it contains most of the nouns, verb endings and sentence patterns introduced so far.

Note. Pleading mitigating circumstances and appealing to the pity of judges was a regular feature of defence in Roman courts.

Illustrations.

p. 122 Mosaic of squid in women's changing room (*Forum Baths, Herculaneum*), as is the octopus, p. 128. Marine motifs were popular for baths and the simplicity of black and white, rather than coloured, mosaic produced a crisp and vivid effect.

p. 123 • Women's changing room (*Stabian Baths, Pompeii*) with recesses for clothing. Behind the photographer is a small cold-water tank; unlike the men, Pompeian women did not have a separate frigidarium.
      • Reconstruction of men's hot room (*Forum Baths, Pompeii*).

Cultural background material (pp. 124–7)

Content. The text and picture essay describe a visit to the baths. The different rooms, activities and heating system are explored in some detail.

Discussion. One way of approaching the information is to start with the picture essay, and encourage students to support their own observations by referring to the text.

The technical terms for the different areas of the baths can be hard for some students to remember. A lively, if somewhat noisy, activity to help younger students with this is to label different areas of the classroom and have students visit the different rooms and enact what took place in them.

Further information. Some details in the students' material are particular to the baths in Pompeii, and some are general features.

Baths were a popular and fashionable meeting place in Roman life, providing both public hygiene and a lively social centre. Critics saw them as an indication of social decadence like extravagant dinner parties; some were a cover for prostitution.

The main hours of bathing were in the afternoon; women (and elderly people) went in the morning to baths which did not have separate provision. Most baths were run as commercial enterprises by individuals who hired the lease for a period of time. The hirer appointed a superintendent and charged a modest entrance fee.

Illustrations

p. 124 Bathers would carry a set of strigils with differing curvature, and a small flask of oil (*Naples, Archaeological Museum*).

p. 125 Picture essay, suggesting bather's route round the baths:
(1) Rich stucco decoration in men's Stabian Baths, Pompeii.
(2) In the tepidarium of the men's Forum Baths, Pompeii, a brazier with bronze benches grouped round it can be seen at the rear behind a modern grille. Heating the warm room by brazier instead of underfloor heating was outdated by AD 79, but was still in operation at the Forum Baths while the Stabian Baths were out of use for modernisation.
(3, 4) Women's Forum Baths, Herculaneum. Notice in 3 the grooved ceiling to channel condensation down the walls.
(5) Men's Forum Baths, Pompeii.

p. 126 The bronze boxer, found on the site of the Baths of Constantine, Rome, has a scarred face with blood oozing from cuts. He wears the Roman form of boxing-gloves, and arm bands to wipe sweat and blood out of his eyes (*Rome, Museo Nazionale Romano*).

p. 127 • Hypocaust, tepidarium of men's Stabian Baths (pictured on p. 117). The diagram beside it is a generalised representation. In fact, in the Stabian Baths, the hot air rose up the walls behind tiles with built-in spacers at the corners (not visible in this picture) rather than the box flues familiar from Roman sites in Britain. The arched hole behind the water tank (towards top right of photograph) would have led to a half-cylindrical tank, with its flat side supported above a small fire to keep the water hot (see pictures pp. 61–7 in *Pompeii* by P. Connolly).
• Plan of Forum Baths, Pompeii, with light blue representing water (bathing tanks and boilers). It is not quite accurate on the men's side, where a brazier was still being used (see note to p. 125), but reflects what became standard Roman practice as an example of Roman practical efficiency.

p. 128 Octopus, women's Forum Baths, Herculaneum (cf. p. 122).

Suggested activities

1 Ask students to design and label their own set of baths, perhaps on computer.
2 *Worksheet Master* 9.5 is a picture exercise, linking the plan of the baths, the rooms and the activities that took place in them.

STAGE 10 rhētor

Cultural background	Story line	Main language features	Focus of exercises
The Roman education system; books and writing.	At the rhetor's, Quintus and his Greek friend, Alexander, debate the respective merits of the Romans and the Greeks. Quintus resolves a quarrel between Alexander's two young brothers. Story about a magic ring and the consequences of owning it.	• 1st and 2nd person plural present including **esse**. • Comparative.	1 1st person plural of present. 2 Nominative complements in 1st and 2nd person plural sentences.

Opening page (p. 129)

Illustration. Marble statue of an elderly Greek teaching. Students might like to look at his hand and suggest what he is saying, e.g. 'Listen to this', or 'There are four points', or **nōs Graecī Rōmānōs docēmus** (p. 133). It is in fact the philosopher Chrysippus (*c*.280–207 BC), a prominent member of the Stoic school of philosophers, whose teachings were studied and followed by many educated Romans. He is included here as a symbol of the important part that Greeks played in Roman education. The statue is now in the Louvre, though the head is a cast of one in the British Museum (*Photograph Giraudon*).

Model sentences (pp. 130–3)

New language feature. 1st and 2nd person plural of the present (including **esse**).

New vocabulary. architectī, pontēs, aedificāmus, fundōs, sculptōrēs, barbarī, ūtilēs, quam (*than*).

First reading. Set the scene of a debate, and make it clear that:
1 One speaker puts forward claims about the merits of the Romans, the other advances the Greek case.
2 The task of the class is to discover the claims and criticisms made on each side.
   Students with a knowledge of French, Spanish or Italian have little difficulty with **nōs** and **vōs**; for others the introductory sentences (**Rōmānus dīcit/Graecus dīcit**) provide the clue.

Illustrations. The pictures contain a good deal of detail and it is helpful to discuss each one for a few moments before tackling the caption:

1 Surveying along a road for a public building, using a **grōma** and poles. A surveyor would plant the stake of the groma firmly in the ground, check by the plumb-lines that it was absolutely upright, and look along the arms to mark out a straight line or along the cords to mark out a right angle.

2 Country estate with pigs and cattle. Note the terracing, and the plough drawn by oxen wearing a yoke.

3 Making a copy of a Greek marble statue. The apparatus at the right would have been used to measure the height at key points of the statue to ensure that the copy was accurate.

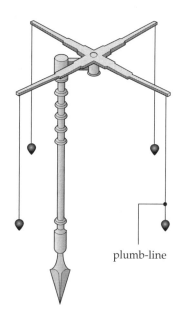

plumb-line

4 Painting murals. The wall was prepared with three coats of fine polished plaster. The painting was done while the surface was still wet, so that the colours were absorbed into the plaster. The paints were made from powdered minerals mixed with egg or honey, made up as required.

5 Greek engrossed in a play, while his fellows sleep.

6 Roman legionaries fighting barbarians. The Romans are wearing helmets designed to protect their necks, cheeks and noses and body armour made of strips of metal; they carry rectangular shields and swords. Note their disciplined formation and their efficient sword technique in contrast with that of the barbarians.

7 Installing a public lavatory; putting in stone seating at back, adjusting a tap at front. Note the lack of privacy.

8 Teacher and class.

Consolidation. The sentences draw a contrast between Greek intellectual and artistic skills and Roman practicality. Draw this out in discussion by asking students what difference they notice in the *kind* of things the two nations are proud of.

contrōversia (pp. 134–5)

Story. The rhetor sets as a debating topic 'Greeks are better than Romans'. Quintus and his friend Alexander take opposing sides. Quintus earns the applause of the other students but Alexander is judged by the teacher to have made the better case.

First reading. This story contains little action. Although the arguments are presented in simple and fairly concrete terms, it can go flat unless you help the class to understand:

1 The more abstract words and phrases, e.g. **nōs tamen nōn sententiam quaerimus**, **nōs argūmentum quaerimus** (lines 11–12) and **Graeciōrēs quam nōs Graecī** (lines 30–1).

2 The formality of an exercise intended to prepare well-to-do young men for the duties of politics and the law courts. The *Independent Learning Manual* Stage 10 suggests a practical way of helping students to assess the quality of the arguments used.

3 The emotional involvement of the speakers in their arguments, which express their cultural and national identity and racial prejudices.

4 The interest in this topic in Pompeii, with its history of a mixed Greek and Roman population. Note that the teacher would have been a Greek himself, perhaps a freedman.

Some possible questions are:

Why did the class applaud Quintus?

Why was it Alexander who replied to Quintus?

At line 31 (before reading the rest of the story): Who do you think should win the debate? Why?

Do you agree with Theodorus' verdict? Could he be accused of bias?

Consolidation. In discussion, some of the historical and cultural references in the two speeches may be explained, and the examples considered. The examples given by Quintus and Alexander follow the argument in the model sentences and are further illustrated by the photographs; the Romans are the practical ones, the Greeks the men of ideas. Discuss whether this is an over-simplification.

Students may enjoy their own debate on the subject. Divide the class into Greeks and Romans and ask them to put forward their cases based on the story and the model sentences.

Illustrations

p. 135 • The bridge at Alcantara was built around AD 106 and has been considered the finest bridge in the Roman world. It is almost 200 metres long and the arches rise nearly 50 metres above the River Tagus. It is constructed in stone, without mortar. Roman architecture is famous for the skilful use of arches in bridges, aqueducts and buildings such as the Colosseum.

• Marble portrait of Euripides (485?–406? BC). The head looks too small because the statue is actually a composite; a head of Euripides is attached to the body of an unidentified dramatist holding a tragic mask (*Rome, Vatican Museums*).

• Mosaic of Anaximander of Miletus, born 610 BC (*Trier, Rheinisches Landesmuseum*).

About the language 1 (p. 136)

New language feature. 1st and 2nd person plural. All persons of the present tense (including **esse**) have now been met and are tabulated here.

Discussion. Depending upon the confidence shown by students, you may find it necessary to tackle the note in three parts: paragraphs 1–2, 3–4 and 5–6. If so, it is sensible to postpone 3–4 until **statuae** has been read, since it contains more examples of the 1st and 2nd person plural with the pronoun omitted.

Begin by using the same technique as that in Stage 4 (p. 42 of this Guide) and then proceed to the note.

Consolidation. This could include:
1 Oral practice of 1st and 2nd person plural of common verbs, initially with **nōs** and **vōs**, then dropping the pronoun. Then practise the whole of the present tense, again phasing the pronouns out gradually.
2 Exercises in 'Practising the language' (p. 140) and *Worksheet Master* 10.2.

**statuae (p. 137)

Story. Quintus goes home with Alexander, who on the way buys some statuettes as birthday presents for his young brothers. As they quarrel over who should receive which statuette, Quintus demonstrates Roman peacemaking skills by allocating to each brother the statuette suited to his disposition, and keeping one for himself.

First reading. Take the passage at a brisk pace, bringing out the contrast between the petulance of the small boys and the comparative maturity of the others. Many students will admit similar experience of young siblings.

Consolidation. Ask students to pick out examples of 1st and 2nd person plural. Discuss examples where the pronouns are omitted (lines 24 and 34). If you have not already done so, read paragraphs 3–4 of 'About the language', p. 136.

Illustration. Three small terracotta statuettes (*Taranto, Museo Nazionale Archeologico*).

About the language 2 (p. 138)

New language feature. The comparative. The superlative was explained in Stage 8. This note should present no difficulties as the comparative has become familiar from the arguments in this Stage, but make a point of discussing the difference between singular and plural forms.

Consolidation. Students enjoy going back through the stories to see how many examples they can find. *Worksheet Master* 10.4 is an exercise on comparatives and superlatives.

ānulus Aegyptius (pp. 138–9)

Story. An antique Egyptian ring stolen from a pyramid brings ill-luck to those who receive it, and ends up with Grumio and Poppaea.

First reading. With more able students, try breaking off your reading in Latin to ask the class who has the ring at each particular moment. They enjoy working out the answer, and it is a good aural comprehension exercise.

Note that from now on **est** is also found in the final position, e.g. **ānulus antīquus est**.

The passage contains a range of language features including: shifts between present and past time, perfect and imperfect tenses, **quod** and **postquam** clauses, and many examples of the dative case. Give students enough time and help with the first reading to ensure that they can attempt the comprehension questions successfully. The answers and mark scheme are as follows. Give credit for any sensible answer.

		Marks
1	With a ring.	1
2	Because he had no money.	1
3	His ship had been wrecked/lost at sea.	2
4	The ring is old. An Egyptian slave gave it to him. The slave found it in a pyramid.	3
5	The innkeeper showed and gave the ring to his wife.	2
6	A huge slave.	1
	He made her hand over the money and the ring.	2
7	The inn was on fire.	1
8	The slaves (began to) beat him up; he fled; he lost the ring.	3
9	Grumio.	1
10	The innkeeper.	1
	The innkeeper, because the ring had brought bad luck to all the previous owners: Syphax, the innkeeper's wife, the innkeeper himself, and the huge slave. *Or* Poppaea, because the ring might be valuable if it was old and unusual.	2
		TOTAL 20

Illustration. Bronze ring, decorated with heads of the Egyptian gods Isis and Serapis (*British Museum*). Care has been taken not to show a gold ring, as at this time the wearing of gold rings was restricted by law to senators and members of the order of Roman Knights (**equitēs**). If Grumio had been found wearing one it would definitely not have been his lucky day.

Practising the language (p. 140)

Exercise 1. Completing sentence with verb in 1st person plural according to sense. You may need to discuss the meaning of the phrases in brackets before students write out the exercise.

Exercise 2. Completing sentence containing **sumus** or **estis** with an appropriate nominative according to sense.

Language information: revision

With the introduction of the dative in Stage 9, students have met all the cases of the noun presented in Book I. This is a good time to revise the noun tables and the uses of the cases set out on p. 180 and to work through the exercises on p. 181.

Cultural background material (pp. 140–3)

Content. An outline of the Roman educational system, and the preparation it gave for adult life.

Discussion. Take the material in two stages: the earliest phase of education and the tools for reading and writing; then the skills developed in the later phases and the activities in public life for which they were a preparation.

Discussion might focus on the differences and similarities between Roman and modern education, including the purpose of education.

Illustrations

p. 141 • Line drawings of writing materials. See also the information given on p. 40 of this Guide.

• A well-preserved wax tablet of the 2nd century AD. The line the schoolboy has had to write out is from the poet Menander: 'Accept advice from a wise man' – an appropriate copybook precept. Notice the lines ruled to guide the pupil (*British Library, Add. MS 341187(1)II*).

p. 142 • A stone relief of the 3rd century AD showing a school scene from Neumagen, Germany. The teacher is shown bearded in the Greek manner; he has a footstool. Two pupils sit in high-backed chairs while a third seems to be arriving late, carrying a satchel which would contain his tablets, stilus and so on (*Trier, Rheinisches Landesmuseum*).

• A poorly preserved painting from the series of forum scenes in the house of Julia Felix at Pompeii (cf. pp. 48–9; also note on p. 42 of this Guide). We can make out the forum colonnade with its garlands hanging between the columns. Pupils (one barely visible) sit at left while a schoolmaster (right) flogs a boy who is supported on the back of another student. The standing figures (centre left) could be bystanders in the forum (*Naples, Archaeological Museum*).

p. 143 • In this 3rd century AD mosaic, Virgil is seen composing the *Aeneid*, flanked by Clio, the muse of history (left) and Melpomene, the muse of tragedy (*Tunis, Bardo Museum*).

• Carving a table leg: marble relief, detail from 3rd century AD sarcophagus (*Rome, Vatican Museums*).

p. 144 Writing materials: detail from Pompeian wall-painting. The title label can be seen hanging from the papyrus roll, and a dot in the centre of the open pages of the wax tablet represents a raised stud sometimes left in the middle of a page to prevent the two wax surfaces rubbing against each other when the tablet was closed (*Naples, Archaeological Museum*).

Suggested activities

1 Write a school report for Quintus (or a younger girl or boy in Pompeii). See *Worksheet Master* 10.3 for suggestions.

2 *Worksheet Master* 10.6 is a simple exercise on Roman writing materials.

3 If there is time, students may enjoy learning the Greek alphabet and transliterating some Greek and English words. See *Worksheet Master* 10.5.

STAGE 11 candidātī

Cultural background	Story line	Main language features	Focus of exercises
Pompeii: elections and local government.	The Tullii brothers support different candidates in the election and make use of the services of a sign-writer. Grumio finds a way of taking part in the elections, at some cost to himself.	• Intransitive verbs with dative. • Sentence pattern NOMINATIVE + DATIVE + VERB. • **placet**. • **nōbīs** and **vōbīs**. • Different ways of asking questions: **quis**, **quid**, etc. no interrogative **-ne**.	1 Selection of verb in correct person. 2 Selection of noun in correct case.

Opening page (p. 145)

Illustration. This marble statue from the junction of the Via dell' Abbondanza and the Via di Stabia shows the most famous of the Holconii, Marcus Holconius Rufus, in military dress (*Naples, Archaeological Museum*). Somewhat earlier than the Holconius of this Stage, he held the duovirate five times at Pompeii, served in the Roman army and had a career in Rome. He was described as **patrōnus** of the town of Pompeii, and paid for improvements to the Temple of Apollo and the Great Theatre.

Model sentences (pp. 146–7)

New language feature. A new sentence pattern NOMINATIVE + DATIVE + VERB in which the dative is used in the following ways:
1 With **faveō** and **crēdō**, e.g. **nōs Lūciō favēmus**.
2 With a verb of replying, e.g. **mercātōrēs agricolīs respondent**.

New vocabulary. candidātōs, noster, favēmus, crēdimus.

First reading. Students might query the dative, asking, for instance, why *merchant* is not in the accusative in **nōs mercātōrī favēmus**. Suggest that **favēmus** corresponds to the English *We give our support* and ask how the sentence should be finished. If the question is not raised, postpone any explanation until 'About the language 1' (p. 150).

Marcus et Quārtus (p. 148)

Story. Two brothers are arguing about the best candidate: Marcus supports Afer, a wealthy property owner; Quartus prefers Holconius because he is of noble birth and the Tullii have traditionally supported the Holconii. Quartus pays a sign-writer 10 denarii to paint a slogan on the house wall in support of Holconius.

First reading. This story and the next should be planned together. Study the first page of the background information (p. 156) as a preliminary to the stories, to give students a realistic context.

There are some useful comprehension questions in the *Independent Learning Manual* Stage 11. Introduce suspense at the end of this story by emphasising in your Latin reading **mihi** in line 22, and invite students to suggest the sequel.

placetne tibi (line 21) and **mihi placet** (line 22): encourage a range of natural English translations, e.g., for **placetne tibi?** *Does that suit you?* or *Will that do for you?* or *Is that all right for you?*

Consolidation. Oral practice of the new language features in the story is useful preparation for the next story. Alternatively, discuss 'About the language 1', paragraphs 1–4, if students are dealing confidently with **faveō** and **crēdō**.

Sulla (p. 149)

Story. Marcus makes the sign-writer wipe out the pro-Holconius slogan and pays him to replace it with one supporting Afer. When Quartus objects, Sulla paints two signs, pleasing both brothers and earning 30 denarii.

First reading. Possible questions might be:
Why was Marcus angry (line 2)?
Was the slogan completely true (lines 11–12)?
Why did Marcus want the words **et frāter** included?
How much money did Sulla make from the brothers altogether (line 28)?

About the language 1 (p. 150)

New language feature. faveō etc. with dative; the dative with the impersonal **placet**; and the dative form of **nōs** and **vōs**.

Discussion. If paragraphs 1–4 were taken after 'Marcus et Quārtus', a few fresh examples should give sufficient practice.

Consolidation. Ask students to pick out examples of **placet** in the two stories and to work out the most appropriate English translation according to the situation and the person speaking.

**Lūcius Spurius Pompōniānus (pp. 151–3)

These four scenes of knockabout comedy give revision practice in the present tense, and accusative and dative cases. They should be given a first reading at a brisk pace. If time is short, they can be omitted or postponed until a Friday afternoon, when the class could be divided into four groups, each acting a scene.

in vīllā (p. 151)

Play. Grumio sets off for the hustings in the guise of a Roman citizen. Clemens goes with him because he is worried about the risk Grumio is taking.

First reading. Some useful questions:
> Why does Clemens think that Grumio ought to support Holconius?
> Why does Grumio support Afer?
> When Grumio calls himself Lucius Spurius Pomponianus, why does he give himself three names?
> Why does Clemens describe Grumio's plan as **perīculōsam** (line 22)?

prope amphitheātrum (p. 152)

Play. Grumio is pleased to be given 5 denarii by Afer's election agent, but disconcerted to be handed a club.

First reading. Some useful questions:
> On which word of Grumio's speech, **salvē** … **sumus** (lines 4–6), does he thump Clemens? Why?
> Why does Grumio describe himself and Afer as **amīcissimī**?
> What does Grumio receive in addition to the denarii? Why?

in forō (pp. 152–3)

Play. Grumio and Clemens join the bakers who are conducting Afer to the forum. They are perturbed to spot Caecilius with Holconius, and Grumio flees. A fight breaks out between the parties.

First reading. How does Grumio's tone of voice change during his speech, **euge**! … **ad vīllam reveniō!** (lines 7–9)?

Consolidation. Ask students to pick out and translate the comparatives and the superlative in the story: **melior** (lines 3 and 13); **fortiōrēs** (line 24); **fortissimī** (line 21).

Note. There is a speech made by Holconius in *Worksheet Master* 11.3.

in culīnā (p. 153)

Play. Grumio tells Clemens he was mistaken for a baker because of the club, beaten up by the opposition and relieved of the 5 denarii. Clemens displays the 10 denarii given him for rescuing Caecilius from the fight, and goes off to meet Poppaea at the harbour.

First reading. Some useful questions:

1 In what state is Grumio's toga now? What state was it in at the start? How do you know?
2 Why did the merchants describe Grumio as **fortis** (line 5) when they saw him in the forum?
3 Where had Grumio obtained the denarii which the merchants seized from him?
4 In what way has Poppaea apparently changed her affections? Can you suggest a reason?
5 Do you feel sorry for Grumio at the end? Or do you feel he deserved what he got?

Consolidation. *Worksheet Master* 11.2 has the conversation between Poppaea and Clemens when they meet, and is a revision exercise of the nominative, accusative and dative cases.

Note. When students have completed their work on these scenes, ask them to predict the result of the election. Then tell them that in the elections to the duovirate in Pompeii in AD 79, the victorious candidates were M. Holconius Priscus and C. Cerrinus Vatia.

Illustration. The photograph shows the speaker's platform on the west side of the forum, near the Temple of Apollo. In the background at left is the colonnade fronting Eumachia's Clothworkers' Guildhall.

About the language 2 (p. 154)

New language feature. Questions.

Discussion. As the note summarises the types of question met so far there should be no problems. **num** is not mentioned here. It should be treated as a vocabulary item *surely … not?* when encountered in stories and not discussed further unless students ask.

Consolidation. Repeated spells of 5-minute oral practice of the questioning words, and question-spotting in future stories are both useful. Ask students to reply (in Latin, if possible) to simple oral questions in Latin, e.g. **quis es? ubi habitās?**

Practising the language (p. 155)

Exercise 1. Selection of verb in correct person.
Exercise 2. Selection of noun in correct case or number (examples are restricted to nominative and accusative). Point out that two language points are practised here.

Language information: revision

pp. 186–7 'Word order' and p. 188 'Longer sentences with **postquam** and **quod**' can be used as oral exercises or set for homework.

Cultural background material (pp. 156–9)

Content. The system of local government and the way in which Roman values of public service influenced small-town life.

Discussion. The material divides into three sections: general introduction (p. 156); the tradition of public service (p. 157) and election notices (pp. 158–9). Read p. 156 before embarking on the stories and discuss the other sections at convenient points.

Further information. Local government in Pompeii was based on elective officers. Competition was lively, especially for the post of aedile, since appointment as duovir followed almost automatically. A magistrate took office in July, after success at the polls in March. When the eruption occurred, the duoviri had been in post for about a month and the town was still plastered with electoral propaganda.

Illustrations

p. 156 • The westernmost of the three municipal offices (7 on the air photograph, p. 51), which was probably the **cūria** or meeting place of the decurions, who formed the local senate. At the end is an apse where the presiding officials would have sat; the recesses were probably intended for statues. The scaffolding-holes visible in the brickwork were designed to be concealed by a marble facing.

• A wall-painting from Pompeii that may show a bakery, but the toga worn by the man behind the counter makes it more likely that he is an official or candidate for office distributing free bread to the people. The circular loaves on the counter are similar to the one shown on p. 24 (*Naples, Archaeological Museum*).

p. 157 • Temple of Fortuna Augusta. The walls of the **cella** (the room housing the god's statue) survive, as do the steps leading up to them, flanking an altar in the middle. We have to imagine the row of columns that originally ran in front of the cella and supported the gabled roof. The wooden railing is modern.

• Front view of statue of M. Holconius Rufus (see p. 145).

p. 158 This electoral notice reads
CN HELVIVM SABINVM AED D R P O V F
Cnaeum Helvium Sabinum aedilem dignum re publica oramus vos faciatis.
We beg you to make Cnaeus Helvius Sabinus aedile. He is worthy of public office.

p. 159 This illustration is based on inscriptions found on the wall of the house of Trebius Valens. The inscriptions are (clockwise from top left):

- Gaium Iulium Polybium aedilem viis aedibus sacris publicis procurandis.
  (Vote for) *Gaius Iulius Polybius as aedile for supervising roads, temples and public works.*
- Decimi Lucreti Satri Valentis flaminis gladiatorum paria decem pugnabunt.
  Ten pairs of gladiators owned by Decimus Lucretius Satrius Valens, priest (in the cult of the Emperor Nero), *will fight.*
- lanternari tene scalam.
  Hold on to the ladder, lantern-bearer.
- Quintum Postumium Modestum.
  (Vote for) *Quintus Postumius Modestus.*
- Gnaeum Helvium Sabinum aedilem oramus faciatis.
  Lucium Ceium Secundum duovirum oramus faciatis.
  We beg you to make Gnaeus Helvius Sabinus aedile.
  We beg you to make Lucius Ceius Secundus duovir.
- Marcum Holconium duovirum iure dicundo dignum re publica oramus vos faciatis.
  We beg you to make Marcus Holconius duovir for administering justice; he is worthy of public office.

p. 160 Another electoral notice:
  L CEIUM SECVNDVM AED ORPHAEVS FACIT
  Lucium Ceium Secundum aedilem Orphaeus facit.
  Orphaeus makes L. Ceius Secundus aedile.

Suggested activities

1 Hold a mock election, using the information in the Stage to put forward candidates, slogans, graffiti, speeches etc. Alternatively, dramatise the Latin election speech in *Worksheet Master* 11.3.
2 Examine some of the Pompeian graffiti, e.g. on p. 159 or in *Worksheet Master* 11.4.
3 Local government quiz in *Independent Learning Manual* Stage 11.

STAGE 12 Vesuvius

Cultural background	Story line	Main language features
The eruption of Vesuvius, 24 August AD 79; the destruction and excavation of Pompeii.	While Caecilius is dining with Iulius, Clemens comes to summon his master home because of the eruption. On the way home Clemens is delayed because he carries Iulius to safety. He arrives home to find the family missing and Caecilius dying. Caecilius frees Clemens, giving him his signet ring for Quintus.	• 1st and 2nd person (singular and plural) imperfect and perfect. • Imperfect of **esse**.

Opening page (p. 161)

Introduction. Set the context by studying the picture of Vesuvius on this page, the line drawings on p. 162 and the picture essay on p. 171. Identify the phenomena associated with recorded eruptions, e.g. rumblings, mushroom cloud, lava, ash, fire. Other useful points for discussion are:

1 The behaviour of people in the picture on p. 161.
2 The physical dominance of the mountain in the streets and squares of Pompeii.
3 The distance of Pompeii from the mountain (see map, p. 172).
4 The attraction of living on the slopes of volcanic mountains (fertile soil, family tradition, etc.).

Illustration. Here people are fleeing from an eruption of Vesuvius on 8 August 1779 (engraving by Francesco Piranesi coloured by Jean-Louis Desprez). The mountain was very active from 1631 until its last eruption in 1944. In this picture the remains of its old cone can be seen, with the new one glowing within it (*British Museum, Department of Prints and Drawings*).

Model sentences (pp. 162–3)

New language feature. 1st and 2nd person singular and plural of both past tenses. The perfect and imperfect tenses are mostly shown side by side, as in Stage 6, the imperfect representing a continuous situation and the perfect an event which is fully realised. Pronouns are used as markers at first, and gradually withdrawn in this and later Stages.

New vocabulary. sonōs, **tremōrēs**, **sēnsī**, **nūbem**, **cinerem**, **flammās**.

First reading. If necessary, remind students of the minor characters they met a while ago: Syphax and Celer (Stage 3, pp. 28–31); Lucrio and Poppaea (Stage 5, p. 61).

tremōrēs (pp. 164–5)

Story. Caecilius is discussing the eruption over dinner at Iulius' house near Nuceria. To his surprise, Clemens, whom he had sent to his farm in the country, arrives from Pompeii asking for him.

First reading. Students become so concerned to find out what happens during the eruption that they are likely to set a fast pace for the first reading of the stories in this Stage until they reach the climax. Give support by dramatic Latin reading, judicious section breaks, assistance with vocabulary and pointed questions. Little help is usually required with the new structures.

Caecilius rented a farm, the Fundus Audianus, for 6,000 sesterces. We know from three surviving tablets that he found it difficult to pay the rent.

Consolidation. The comprehension questions are suitable for group work. Ask students to produce written answers. The answers and mark scheme are as follows. Accept any sensible answer.

		Marks
1	Caecilius was dining with Iulius. He was in Iulius' (splendid) house near Nuceria.	2
2	He had felt tremors/The earth had trembled.	1
3	He was dictating letters to a slave.	1
4	A strange cloud.	1
5	He had called his household to the shrine and they had sacrificed to the gods.	2
6	They had felt tremors and had seen the cloud, but were not terrified.	3
7	A long time ago there had been earth tremors, and walls and houses had been destroyed, but the gods had saved him and his household.	3
8	Clemens was in the atrium; he had come from the city and was looking for Caecilius.	3
9	He was puzzled. He had sent Clemens to the farm that morning.	2
10	Clemens had been alarmed by the tremors and reports of panic in Pompeii/He had been sent by the family, who were worried about Caecilius' safety, etc.	2
	TOTAL	20

Illustrations

pp. 164–5 The reliefs were found on the lararium in Caecilius' house and show the effects of the earthquake in AD 62. Both reliefs appear to relate to his own experiences, and may have been put up in gratitude for his preservation. The left-hand panel shows a scene that would have been visible from Caecilius' front door. From left:

- The water reservoir that supplied the street fountains, public baths and some private houses.
- The Vesuvius Gate.
- A stretch of city wall with a cart drawn by two mules in front. Right-hand panel:
- Honorific arch flanking the Temple of Jupiter in the forum, with equestrian statues on either side of the temple, and the altar in front.

p. 165 Bronze statuette of a lar, typically shown as a young man with billowing clothes, holding a shallow bowl for drink-offerings in one hand and a drinking-horn in the other. Shrines for the lares were sometimes in the kitchen, since they ensured that the family had plenty to eat and drink (*Oxford, Ashmolean Museum*).

ad urbem (p. 166)

Story. Clemens explains that he and the farm manager felt too afraid to stay on the farm. He found Metella and Quintus very worried, and was sent to fetch Caecilius. On his way home, Caecilius meets Holconius fleeing to the harbour, and is shocked by his lack of concern for Metella.

First reading. Keep the story moving by dramatic Latin reading, and by breaking it down into sections at points where students will want to continue, e.g.:

'quid vōs fēcistis?' rogāvit Iūlius (line 6).
'… perterritī erāmus.' (line 13).
'cūr nōn ad portum fugitis?' rogāvit Holcōnius (lines 19–20).

Consolidation. Stress the perfect forms of verbs such as **āmittere**, **dēlēre**, **contendere** and **cōnspicere**.

If students are dealing confidently with the new persons of the verb, take 'About the language' (p. 170) at this point. Students will thus have a chance to become thoroughly familiar with these forms before undertaking a general revision of verbs from the 'Language information' section.

ad vīllam (p. 167)

Story. Caecilius finds Pompeii in chaos. His friend Iulius collapses. Clemens carries Iulius to the sanctuary of the Temple of Isis, where he eventually recovers. Clemens refuses to flee with Iulius, preferring to follow Caecilius in the search for his family.

First reading. Again let the dramatic points of the narrative dictate the end of the sections you select for students to explore, e.g.:

statim ad terram dēcidit exanimātus (line 8).
Clēmēns cum Iūliō in templō manēbat (line 13).

Be prepared to help at lines 15–16 where **sumus** is introduced without **nōs**.

Consolidation. Possible discussion points:
Why did Iulius collapse? (Sulphur fumes are mentioned on p. 172.)
Why did Caecilius leave the temple? Why did Iulius call him
stultissimus?
Why did Iulius decide to leave the city?
Why did Clemens follow Caecilius?

Illustrations

- Bezel of a gold ring (enlarged) showing a bust of Isis, wearing a vulture headdress supporting the cow horns and disc of the Egyptian goddess Hathor, with whom she was identified in the Graeco-Roman world (she was 'Isis of countless names'). Hathor, like Isis, was a nurturing, protective deity (*Victoria and Albert Museum*).
- Temple of Isis seen from its surrounding colonnade. Between the columns on the left can be glimpsed the entrance to a shrine which contained a pool of sacred water, representing the Nile.

fīnis, (pp. 168–9)

Story. After struggling through the city, Clemens reaches home to find it in ruins with Cerberus guarding his dying master. Caecilius orders Clemens to flee and to deliver his signet ring to Quintus, if he finds him.

First reading. Read the first two lines in Latin to establish the sombre atmosphere of this final story and then invite interpretations. The shifts in mood at lines 8–9 (… **dominum custōdiēbat**) and line 19 (**Clēmēns recūsāvit**) suggest appropriate sections for exploration.

Consolidation. Possible topics for discussion include:
Which words depict the behaviour of the volcano at this time?
Find words which show Clemens' feelings. Does his mood change?
Why is the ring (line 22) important?
Which is the most significant word in the last two sentences?
The fate of the historical Caecilius is not known. Students often ask what happens to the rest of the household. The answer should be kept for Book II (where Clemens and Quintus reappear).

Illustration

Some of the casts made by pouring plaster into the impressions in the ash left by decomposing bodies: children, adults and a dog. The dog must have been struggling to free himself from his chain, hence his contorted position. Some of the people seem to have died quite peacefully, recalling the Younger Pliny's statement that his uncle's body, when found after the eruption, looked 'more like a man asleep than dead' (*Letters* VI.16). The skeletons of others, not shown here, have been found torn apart by violent pyroclastic flows.

About the language (pp. 170–1)

New language features. 1st and 2nd person singular and plural of the imperfect and perfect tenses; tabulation of the full imperfect and perfect tenses; the imperfect of **esse**.

Discussion. Start by putting on the board or OHP some paired examples of imperfects and perfects based on the model sentences, e.g.:

Syphāx servōs vēndēbat.   frātrēs tremōrēs sēnsērunt.

Syphāx: 'ego servōs vēndēbam.'   Marcus: 'nōs tremōrēs sēnsimus.'

Invite comments and proceed to the language note.

Take the note in two parts, breaking off at the end of paragraph 2 to pick out examples from pp. 166–7 and study them in a familiar context. Then discuss paragraphs 3 and 4, asking students to comment on the easy 'regular' endings and those that are likely to cause problems (generally **-ī**, **-istī**, **-istis**). Finally, see if they can manage the examples in paragraph 5 without reference to p. 170.

Consolidation. Further practice could be based on examples of the 1st and 2nd person of the imperfect and perfect tenses found in the stories of the Stage, e.g.:

1 Ask students to find and translate examples in the text.
2 Vary the person of the examples found, and ask for a translation.
3 Omit the pronoun from some of these examples, and ask for a translation.

Illustrations

- Detail of a painting from Pompeii of the vine-clad mountain. Part of a figure of Bacchus, dressed in grapes, can be seen at left (*Naples, Archaeological Museum*).
- Detail of the engraving on p. 161.
- Steam rising inside the crater. Vesuvius is overdue for an eruption and the crater is constantly monitored for seismic activity.
- The mountain from the sea. The coast is now entirely built up. This congested population will be vulnerable in any future eruption, and the Italian government has already drawn up plans for evacuation. The site of Herculaneum is roughly in the centre of the picture, Pompeii outside it to the right.

Language information: revision

The following work should be postponed until students are confident with all persons of the imperfect and perfect tenses. You may find it more useful for revising verbs in the early Stages of Book II.

pp. 182–4 Revise the three tenses tabulated in paragraph 1 and the meanings given in paragraph 2. Then study paragraphs 3 and 4, which formally introduce the four conjugations. Ask students what similarities and differences they see. The exercise in paragraph 5 is easy and can be done orally, while that in paragraph 6 is a good test of persons and tenses if worked without reference to the table. After revising **sum** and **eram** in paragraph 7, give students written or oral practice with their books closed.

p. 185 Paragraphs 1 and 2 consolidate and extend students' knowledge of present and perfect forms. They should now learn to recognise the regular perfect forms in the 1st, 2nd and 4th conjugations and the examples of irregular perfects. Follow up with examples taken from the stories.

Cultural background material (pp. 172–5)

Content. An account of the destruction of Pompeii in the eruption and the subsequent history of the site.

Discussion. Study this section after the Latin stories have been read. It can be used as an observation exercise, with students being led by the teacher's questions to draw their own deductions from the pictures, and extend them by reference to the text. Possible discussion points:

How do we know that the city came to a sudden end and did not just fade away?

How do archaeologists gather information when they excavate a site?

Further information. The distance of Pompeii from Vesuvius makes the extent of its devastation surprising. The strength and direction of the wind during the eruption may need to be explained with the help of the map (p. 172). The most recent research indicates that the eruption in AD 79 was an explosive eruption, not one with slow-moving lava flows. The best contemporary description is that of Pliny the Younger who was at Misenum (*Letters* VI.16).

Illustrations

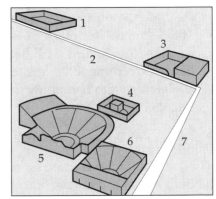

p. 172 Model showing part of Pompeii as excavated (*Naples, Archaeological Museum*). The diagram shows the features to note:

1 Clothworkers' Guildhall
2 The Street of Shops
3 The Stabian Baths
4 The Temple of Isis in its precinct
5 The large theatre
6 The small theatre
7 Stabiae Street

p. 173 • General view of the excavated portion of Herculaneum. In the foreground are some of the large Roman houses on the sea wall. Vesuvius rises in the background above the modern town.

- Looking up to a first-floor apartment in Herculaneum. Most of the street frontage has fallen away. Often upper floors contained flats occupied separately from the ground floor.
- This 18th-century picture of the early excavations comes from a lavish book, *Campi Phlegraei* (1776), published by the British ambassador to Naples, Sir William Hamilton, who was the husband of Nelson's mistress Emma Hamilton and a keen antiquarian. Compare the picture with the photograph on p. 167 of the Temple of Isis as it is today.

p. 174
- A resin cast made on the same principles as the earlier plaster casts. This victim was found in 'Villa B' at Oplontis, near Pompeii.
- One of a number of skeletons of people sheltering in the boat sheds, created from the supporting arches of the sea wall at Herculaneum. The gold wire earrings probably held pearls. Compare the snake's-head bracelets with the one on p. 14. Notice how good her teeth are; she had no cavities because of the local diet of seafoods rich in fluoride (*National Geographic*).

p. 175
- A replanted vineyard in south-east Pompeii, which was largely given over to vineyards and market gardening. The exact pattern of planting was recovered in an excavation by Wilhelmina Jashemsky. The vineyard contained an outdoor triclinium where the owner and his guests could enjoy the wine from the crop.
- A group of casts huddled in the corner of the same vineyard. The crawling child on p. 169 belongs to this group.

p. 176 A lantern, *in situ* in the House of the Menander, Pompeii. It would originally have had a thin sheet of horn to protect the flame.

Suggestions for further work

1 The discovery record (*Independent Learning Manual* Stage 12) is a helpful exercise for students trying to follow the history of the excavations.
2 *Worksheet Master* 12.7, based on Pliny the Younger's letter describing his own experience of the eruption.
3 Research projects on the geophysics of eruptions, or the phenomena of this eruption, or a study of another modern eruption.
4 Show and discuss *In the Shadow of Vesuvius* (*National Geographic video*).

Other illustrations

p. 177 Mosaic of guard dog at entrance to the House of the Tragic Poet, opposite the Forum Baths, Pompeii. Inscription reads CAVE CANEM *Beware of the dog*. Caecilius would have seen this every time he went to the Forum Baths.

Back cover. Vesuvius appears beyond the ruined town. Note the umbrella pines, whose shape was mimicked by the cloud of earth and ash erupting from Vesuvius (see Pliny, *Letters* VI.16).

LANGUAGE SYNOPSIS OF BOOK I

The following synopsis indicates the chief language features introduced in each Stage; it also shows whether each feature is described and/or practised in the current Stage or a later one and/or the 'Language information' (LI) section for Book I. All features not described in the Book I 'Language information' section will be described in the language information sections of later Books.

You can use the synopsis to:

1 Check whether a feature occurring in a Stage's reading material is newly introduced in that Stage.
2 Discover where a particular feature is discussed.
3 Find out the Stage in which a particular feature first occurs.

In addition to the traditional grammatical categories of morphology and syntax, the synopsis includes some of the chief sentence patterns of Book I, printed in capital letters. These are not normally discussed in the Stage language notes, but examples are collected under the heading *Word order* in the 'Language information' section in this and subsequent Books. When you make up extra sentences to practise a language point, it is important that the word order of those sentences should follow a pattern which students have already met; the synopsis is often helpful here.

When reading a Stage with a class, concentrate on the features dealt with in that Stage's language note, rather than attempt to discuss every feature listed here.

Stage	*Language feature*	*Place of language note etc.*
1	word order with and without **est**	1
	nominative singular	2
2	nominative (met in Stage 1) and accusative singular	2, LI
	superlative	8
	NOMINATIVE + ACCUSATIVE + VERB word order	LI
3	nominative and accusative of 1st, 2nd and 3rd declensions	3, LI
	attributive adjective (predicative adjective met in Stage 1)	14, 18
	VERB + NOMINATIVE word order	
4	1st and 2nd person singular present (including **sum**)	4, LI
	mē	9
	questions with **quis, quid, cūr, ubi**	11
	questions with no interrogative word	11
	adest	

Stage	Language feature	*Place of language note etc.*
5	nominative plural	5, LI
	3rd person plural present	5, LI
	two nominatives joined with **et**	LI
	puer	
	abest	
6	3rd person singular and plural, imperfect and perfect (**v**-stems)	6, LI
	erat and **erant**	6, LI
	clauses with **postquam** and **quod**	LI
	two accusatives joined with **et**	LI
	clauses with **ubi** (= where)	
7	ACCUSATIVE + VERB word order (i.e. subject omitted)	7, LI
	perfect tense (other than **v**-stems)	7, LI
	tē	9
	oblique cases of **is**	LI, Book II
8	accusative plural	8, LI
	superlative (met from Stage 2)	8
	hic	19
9	dative singular and plural	9, LI
	nominative, accusative and dative of **ego** and **tū**	9
	NOMINATIVE + DATIVE + ACCUSATIVE + VERB word order	LI
	ille	
	ferō	
10	1st and 2nd person plural present (including **sum**)	10, LI
	comparative adjective	10
	comparison with **quam**	10
	nōbīs and **vōbīs**	11
	questions with **-ne**	11
	imperative singular	19
	two datives joined with **et**	LI
	in + accusative (two examples)	
	eō	

Stage	Language feature	Place of language note etc.
11	intransitive verbs + dative	11
	placet	11
	questions with:	
	quis, **quid** etc. (met from Stage 4)	
	no interrogative word (from Stage 4)	
	-ne (from Stage 10)	11
	nōbīs and **vōbīs** (from Stage 10)	11
	vocative	19
	NOMINATIVE + DATIVE + VERB word order	
	mēcum and **tēcum**	
12	1st and 2nd person singular and plural, imperfect and perfect	12, LI
	1st and 2nd person singular and plural imperfect of **esse**	12, LI
	postquam clauses containing DATIVE + ACCUSATIVE + VERB word order	
	ablative plural in prepositional phrases	

The following terms are introduced in Book I. Numerals indicate the Stage in which each term is first used. LI = Language information section.

Term	Stage	Term	Stage
noun	2	present	6
case	2	imperfect	6
nominative	2	perfect	6
accusative	2	superlative	8
declension	3	dative	9
verb	4	comparative	10
singular	5	conjugation	LI
plural	5	irregular	LI
tense	6		

APPENDIX A: ATTAINMENT TESTS

These tests provide a quick check at periodic intervals on the degree to which:

1 Students have understood the recent material.
2 Less recent work has been properly consolidated.
3 There is any need for remedial work.
4 Difficulties with key vocabulary are impeding progress.

They also give students useful practice in working unaided.

The tests are not intended to discriminate sharply between able and less able students to produce a good 'scatter' of marks (a different set of tests would have to be devised for this). From the teacher's point of view, the total of marks achieved by each student is less significant than students' performance on specific points (see the example following Test 3, pp. 96–7); their answers will often help you in preparing the next section of the year's work, but resist the temptation to follow an attainment test by attempting a hasty revision of all matters shown to need attention.

In the tests the words and phrases in heavy type are either new to students or have occurred infrequently up to the Stage indicated. You may find it unnecessary to give students all these words, but it is unrealistic to expect them to recognise words that they have met only once or twice before.

When you correct the scripts, bear in mind the following points:

1 Any English translation that faithfully reflects the meaning of the Latin is acceptable. Structural equivalence should not be insisted upon.
2 Mistakes of vocabulary and morphology should not be heavily penalised in instances where students have not had long to become familiar with the new words and endings.
3 Students will probably have most difficulty with sentences that show a strong contrast with English structure (e.g. sentences with the subject omitted).

Where students have difficulty, it is sometimes helpful to refer them to familiar sentences containing the point which is causing difficulty (the model sentences are often suitable for this purpose, and then make up further examples for students to translate.

Test 1

To be given to students after Stage 4 has been completed.

ad carcerem
iūdex Hermogenem **convincit**.
    'ego Hermogenem **ad carcerem mittō**', inquit iūdex.
    'ego sum **innocēns**', clāmat Hermogenēs.

'**immō**, tū es mercātor **scelestus**!' respondet iūdex. 'tū **multam** pecūniam dēbēs.'   5

servus mercātōrem scelestum ē basilicā **trahit**. servus mercātōrem ad carcerem dūcit et iānuam **pulsat**. **custōs** iānuam **aperit**. custōs est Grōma. Grōma mercātōrem **statim agnōscit**. Grōma rīdet.

'Hermogenēs est amīcus **veterrimus**', inquit Grōma. 'Hermogenēs vīllam nōn habet. Hermogenēs in carcere **habitat**!'   10

servus rīdet. sed Hermogenēs nōn rīdet. Hermogenēs Grōmam vituperat. Grōma est īrātus. Grōma mercātōrem ad carcerem trahit.

'**cella tua** est **parāta**', inquit Grōma.

Test 2

To be given at the end of Stage 8.

vīlla scelesta
in urbe erat vīlla pulchra. vīlla tamen erat **vacua**, quod **umbra ibi** habitābat. omnēs cīvēs umbram valdē timēbant.

Athēnodōrus ad urbem vēnit et **dē umbrā** audīvit. Athēnodōrus tamen umbrās nōn timēbat, quod erat **philosophus**. vīllam igitur **ēmit**.

postquam **nox** vēnit, Athēnodōrus in ātriō sedēbat. subitō philosophus   5
fragōrem audīvit. **respexit** et umbram **horribilem** vīdit. umbra erat senex et multās **catēnās gerēbat**. umbra, postquam **ingemuit**, ad hortum **lentē** ambulābat. Athēnodōrus quoque ad hortum ambulāvit. postquam Athēnodōrus hortum intrāvit, umbra subitō **ēvānuit**.

tum Athēnodōrus servōs vocāvit. servī **palās** portāvērunt et hortum   10
intrāvērunt. servī, postquam in hortō **fōdērunt, hominem** mortuum **invēnērunt**.

Athēnodōrus hominem **rītē sepelīvit**, quod philosophus erat **benignus**. Athēnodōrus umbram **numquam** iterum vīdit.

Test 3

To be given during or at the end of Stage 12.

vēnātiō
Quīntus amīcum habēbat. amīcus erat Valēns. ōlim Quīntus Valentem **vīsitābat**. Valēns in vīllā magnificā prope montēs habitābat. Quīntus, postquam ātrium intrāvit, amīcum salūtāvit.

'tū **opportūnē** vēnistī', inquit Valēns. 'ego multōs amīcōs ad vēnātiōnem invītāvī. nōs omnēs sumus **parātī**. servī et canēs adsunt. tū   5
quoque venīs?'

'**ita vērō**', respondit Quīntus, 'vēnātiōnēs mē valdē dēlectant.'

tum Valēns amīcō longam **hastam** dedit et omnēs ad montēs contendērunt. magnam silvam intrāvērunt ubi multī **cervī** erant. subitō ingēns **lupus appāruit**. Valentem statim petīvit et superāvit. amīcī et servī   10

et canēs fūgērunt quod valdē timēbant. Quīntus tamen ad lupum fortiter
prōcessit et hastam **ēmīsit**. ecce! lupum necāvit.

Valēns, postquam ad vīllam revēnit, Quīntō statuam splendidam dedit.
statua erat leō. 'ego tibi hanc statuam dō', inquit Valēns, 'quod **vītam**
meam servāvistī. tū es fortior quam leō.'   15

The attainment tests can be used diagnostically. For example, Test 3 could
be used to assess progress as follows:

Vocabulary
prope (line 2), omnēs (5, 8), quoque (6), ubi (9), petīvit (10), tamen (11),
fortior (15).

Noun forms
montēs (2), vēnātiōnēs (7).

Verb forms
vīsitābat (2), vēnistī, venīs (4, 6), invītāvī (5), adsunt (5), dō (14), servāvistī
(15).

Sentence structure
1   Single subject of two verbs:
    Quīntus, tamen, ad lupum … ēmīsit (11–12).
2   Different subjects of two verbs:
    tum Valēns amīcō … contendērunt (8–9).
3   Subject not expressed:
    Valentem … superāvit (10).
    lupum necāvit (12).

postquam clauses
Quīntus, postquam ātrium intrāvit, amīcum salūtāvit (2–3).
Valēns, postquam ad vīllam revēnit, Quīntō statuam splendidam dedit (13).
1   Are any students getting the sentence wrong through treating
    postquam as an adverb?
2   Have they managed the clause containing the dative in the second
    sentence?
3   Are some of the more able students preferring *After Quintus entered the
    atrium* to *Quintus, after he entered the atrium*?

APPENDIX B:
BOOK I VOCABULARY CHECKLIST

The numeral indicates the Stage in whose checklist the word or phrase occurs. Verbs are shown here in their infinitive form for consistency with the corresponding lists in the Teacher's Guides to later Books.

abesse (6)
abīre (10)
accipere (10)
ad (3)
adesse (5)
agere (4)
agitāre (8)
agnōscere (9)
agricola (5)
ambulāre (5)
amīcus (2)
āmittere (12)
ancilla (2)
ānulus (4)
audīre (5)

bibere (3)

callidus (10)
canis (1)
capere (11)
celeriter (9)
cēna (2)
cēnāre (7)
cibus (2)
circumspectāre (3)
cīvis (11)
clāmāre (3)
clāmor (5)
complēre (12)
cōnspicere (7)
cōnsūmere (8)
contendere (5)
contentus (10)
convenīre (11)
coquere (4)

coquus (1)
crēdere (11)
cubiculum (6)
cum (= *with*) (7)
cupere (9)
cūr? (4)
currere (5)
custōdīre (12)

dare (9)
dē (= *about*) (11)
diēs (9)
dominus (2)
dormīre (2)
dūcere (8)
duo (12)

ē (4)
ecce! (3)
ego (4)
ēheu! (4)
emere (6)
ēmittere (9)
epistula (12)
esse (1)
et (3)
eum (8)
exclāmāre (10)
exīre (3)
exspectāre (3)

fābula (5)
facere (7)
facile (8)
favēre (11)
fēmina (5)

ferōciter (6)
ferōx (8)
ferre (9)
festīnāre (6)
fīlius (1)
flamma (12)
fortis (6)
fortiter (12)
frāter (10)
frūstrā (12)
fugere (12)
fundus (12)
fūr (6)

gladius (8)

habēre (4)
habitāre (10)
herī (7)
hic (8)
hodiē (5)
homō (9)
hortus (1)
hospes (9)

iacēre (12)
iam (12)
iānua (3)
igitur (12)
ignāvus (8)
ille (9)
imperium (10)
in (1)
ingēns (7)
inquit (4)
īnspicere (9)

intellegere (7)
intentē (6)
intrāre (2)
invenīre (10)
invītāre (11)
īrātus (3)
īre (11)
iterum (9)
iūdex (4)
iuvenis (5)

labōrāre (1)
lacrimāre (7)
laetus (2)
laudāre (2)
legere (11)
leō (3)
liber (10)
līberālis (11)
lībertus (6)

magnus (3)
manēre (9)
māter (1)
medius (9)
mendāx (4)
mercātor (2)
meus (5)
minimē! (11)
mīrābilis (12)
mittere (12)
mōns (12)
mortuus (7)
mox (9)
multī (5)
multus (5)

mūrus (11)

nārrāre (7)
nāvis (3)
necāre (7)
nihil (7)
nōn (3)
nōs (10)
noster (11)
nunc (11)
nūntiāre (10)
nūntius (8)

offerre (9)
ōlim (6)
omnis (7)
optimē (12)
optimus (5)
ostendere (9)

paene (12)
parāre (7)
parvus (6)
pater (1)
pāx (10)
pecūnia (4)
per (6)
perterritus (4)
pēs (8)
petere (= *attack*) (5)
placēre (11)
plaudere (5)

poēta (4)
porta (8)
portāre (3)
portus (10)
post (9)
postquam (6)
postulāre (8)
prīmus (11)
prōcēdere (9)
prōmittere (11)
prope (7)
puella (5)
puer (8)
pugna (11)
pugnāre (8)
pulcher (9)
pulsāre (6)

quaerere (4)
quam (= *than*) (10)
quis? (4)
quod (6)
quoque (2)

reddere (4)
rēs (6)
respondēre (3)
revenīre (9)
rīdēre (3)
rogāre (7)

saepe (8)

salūtāre (2)
salvē! (3)
sanguis (8)
satis (4)
scrībere (6)
sed (4)
sedēre (1)
semper (10)
senātor (11)
senex (5)
sentīre (12)
servāre (10)
servus (1)
signum (4)
silva (8)
sollicitus (11)
sōlus (10)
spectāculum (8)
spectāre (5)
stāre (5)
statim (8)
stultus (11)
subitō (6)
superāre (6)
surgere (3)
suus (10)

taberna (3)
tacēre (10)
tacitē (7)
tamen (7)
tandem (12)

templum (12)
terra (12)
terrēre (7)
timēre (12)
tōtus (8)
trādere (9)
trēs (12)
tū (4)
tum (6)
turba (5)
tuus (6)

ubi (= *where*) (5)
ūnus (12)
urbs (5)
uxor (10)

valdē (7)
valē! (11)
vehementer (10)
vēndere (6)
venīre (5)
verberāre (11)
via (1)
vidēre (3)
vīnum (3)
vir (11)
vituperāre (6)
vocāre (4)
vōs (10)

BIBLIOGRAPHY

Books

Books marked * are suitable for students. Some of the others are also suitable to refer to under the teacher's guidance. Some recommended out-of-print (OP) books are included as teachers may already possess them or be able to obtain second-hand copies.

Pompeii and Herculaneum

Andrews, I. *Pompeii* (Cambridge UP, 1978)
  Art and History of Pompeii (Bonechi Guides, Italy, 1997)
Bisel, S.C. *The Secrets of Vesuvius* (Hodder and Stoughton, 1990)
Brown, D.M. (ed.) *Pompeii, the Vanished City* (Time Life Books, 1992)
Connolly, P. **Pompeii* (Oxford UP, 1990). Highly recommended.
Deiss, J.J. *Italy's Buried Treasure* (J. Paul Getty Museum, 1995)
Etienne, R. **Pompeii – the Day a City Died* (trans. H. Abrahams, Thames and Hudson, 1992). Recommended.
Everyman *Guide to Naples and Pompeii* (Everyman, 1996)
de Franciscis, A. **Pompeii, Monuments Past and Present* (rev. I. Bragantini, Vision SRL, Rome, 1995). Large format.
  *Pompeii, Herculaneum and the Villa Iovis, Capri (Vision Publications, Rome, 1964)
  Both books are invaluable guides with reconstructions. Available from Hellenic Bookservice and Old Vicarage Publications (addresses below).
Hollinghurst, H. (ed.) *Greeks and Romans* (Heinemann, 1974, OP). Contains useful material on Pompeii.
Maiuri, A. *Pompeii – a Guidebook* (Old Vicarage Publications, 1989)
  Herculaneum – a Guidebook (Old Vicarage Publications, 1989)
Wallace-Hadrill, A. *Houses and Society in Pompeii and Herculaneum* (Princeton UP, 1994)
Wood, N. *The House of the Tragic Poet – a Reconstruction* (N. Wood, 1996, address below). Recommended.

Historical novels

Davis, L. **Shadows in Bronze* (Pan, 1991)
Dillon, E. **The Shadow of Vesuvius* (Faber, 1978, OP)
Wilson, B.K. **Beloved of the Gods* (Constable, 1965, OP)

General

Allen, W.S. *Vox Latina* (Cambridge UP, 1965)
Amery, H. and Vanags, P. **The Time Traveller Book of Rome and the Romans* (Usborne, 1976, 1993)
Balsdon, J.P.V.D. *Life and Leisure in Ancient Rome* (Bodley Head, 1969, OP)

Barrow, R. *Greek and Roman Education (Duckworth, 1996)

Bonner, S.F. *Education in Ancient Rome (Bristol Classical Press, 1977)

Buchanan, I. *Roman Sport and Entertainment (Longman, 1976)

Carcopino, J. Daily Life in Ancient Rome (Penguin, 1991)

Dalby, A. and Grainger, S. *The Classical Cookbook (British Museum Publications, 1996)

Edwards, J. (trans.) The Roman Cookery of Apicius (Rider Books, 1996)

Grant, M. *Gladiators (Barnes and Noble, new edn, 1996)

Hamey, L.A. and J.A. *The Roman Engineers (Cambridge UP, 1981)

Hodge, P. *The Roman House (Longman, 1975)
    Roman Towns (Longman, 1977)
    Roman Family Life (Longman, 1974, OP)

Jones, P. and Sidwell, K. The World of Rome (Cambridge UP, 1997)

Lewis, N. and Rheinhold, M. (eds.) Roman Civilisation: A Sourcebook. I The Republic; II The Empire (Columbia UP, new edn, 1990)

Marrou, H.I. (ed.) A History of Education in Antiquity (Sheed and Ward, 1981)

Massey, M. and Moreland, P. *Slavery in Ancient Rome (Duckworth, 1992)

Massey, M. *Roman Religion (Longman, 1979)

McLeish, K. *Roman Comedy (Duckworth, 1986)

Paoli, U.E. Rome, its People, Life and Customs (Bristol Classical Press, 1990)

Shelton, J-A. As the Romans Did (Oxford UP, 1988)

Taylor, D. *Roman Society (Duckworth, 1991)

Wiedemann, T.E.J. Slavery, Greece and Rome: New Surveys in the Classics No. 19 (Oxford UP, 1987)

Woodman, M. *Food and Cooking in Roman Britain (Corinium Museum, 1983).
    Roman Gardens (Corinium Museum, 1987)

Audio-visual resources

Videos

In the Shadow of Vesuvius. Recent excavations at Herculaneum (including the skeleton shown on p. 174 of Book I), and the seismology of the region. 60 minutes. (National Geographic 1048)

Julia in Urbe Pompeiis. Latin dialogue, live action set 'inside' Nicholas Wood's model of the House of the Tragic Poet, Pompeii. Also contains a version with English commentary. The language of the Latin dialogue is more advanced than Stage 12. (Case Television Ltd/Channel Four Corporation). Available from N. Wood (address below).

CDs

Dalladay, R.L. *100 Pictures of Pompeii.* 100 Kodak Photo-CD images. Booklet of notes (address below).

Film

The Last Days of Pompeii (1935). 16mm. Hire from British Film Institute.

Slides and filmstrips

Each title listed is available as a filmstrip or a slide set, unless otherwise stated.

General

Pompeii. Cambridge Classical Filmstrip 1, filmstrip only, 34 frames, notes; designed to accompany the integrated edition of the *Cambridge Latin Course* Unit I (Cambridge UP, 1983)

Pompeii. Filmstrip only, 45 frames, commentary by M.W. Frederiksen. (Hellenic and Roman Societies' Joint Library, address below)

Furneaux Jordan, R. *Pompeii.* 31 slides (plus title slides), notes. Includes cutaway diagram of Pompeian atrium house. From a series on Roman art and architecture. (Visual Publications, HWA 5/4, address below)

Ball, W. *A Roman House.* Set of 24 slides (no filmstrip), notes. Title misleading; includes shots of houses and public baths at Pompeii and Herculaneum. (Fornasa set 504)

White, H.A.B. *Herculaneum.* 40 slides, notes (address below).

Stage 1

White, H.A.B. *The Pompeian House.* 40 slides, notes.

Dalladay, R.L. *Roman Town Houses.* 16 slides, notes and plans. (C5, address below)
Roman Gardens. 14 slides, notes. (C4)
Roman Women. 17 slides, notes. (C11)

Stage 2

Dalladay, R.L. *Roman Food.* 16 slides, notes. (C6)

Stages 3 and 4

White, H.A.B. *Pompeii: Public buildings and business life.* 40 slides, notes.
Roman Painting. 41 slides, 29 show wall-paintings from the Pompeii area. (Visual Publications, HWA 5a/2, address below)

Dalladay, R.L. *Fashions in walls.* 16 slides on wall decoration, much of it from Pompeii. (C9)

Stage 5

Roman Theatre. 44 slides, notes. Includes all types of Roman theatre, and the head of Sorex from Pompeii. (Visual Publications, ET2)

Stage 6

Dalladay, R.L. *Slavery at Rome.* 26 slides, notes. (C8)

Stage 7

Dalladay, R.L. *Hail and Farewell*. On Roman burial customs, 16 slides, notes. (C7)

Beyond the Tomb. On the afterlife, 16 slides, notes. (C16)

Stage 8

Dalladay, R.L. *Life and Death in the Arena*. 36 slides, notes. Includes the Pompeii amphitheatre, gladiators' barracks, etc. with material from elsewhere in the Roman Empire. (C18)

Stage 9

Dalladay, R.L. *Going to the Baths*. 20 slides plus 4 OHTs, notes. Examples mostly drawn from Pompeii and Herculaneum. (C19)

Stage 10

Dalladay, R.L. *Books and Writing*. 20 slides plus 5 sheets of OHTs (2 on Caecilius' tablets, 1 of Pompeian graffiti), notes. (C45)

White, H.A.B. *Roman Books and Writing Materials*. 32 slides, notes.
The Legacy of Pompeii – Roads and Transport. 36 slides, notes. Detailed study of roads, pavements, drainage, etc.

Addresses

British Film Institute: 21 Stephen Street, London W1 2LN; tel: 0171 255 1444, fax: 0171 580 5830.

R.L. Dalladay: Abbey Cottage, East Cliff, Whitby YO22 4JT; tel/fax: 01947 600443.

Roland Collection, Peasmarsh, East Sussex TN31 6XJ; tel: 01797 230421, fax: 01797 230677.

Hellenic Bookservice: 91 Fortress Road, London NW5 1AG.

Hellenic and Roman Societies' Joint Library: The Senate House, Malet Street, London WC1E 7HU; tel: 0171 862 8709, fax: 0171 862 8735.

Old Vicarage Publications: William Ball, The Old Vicarage, Reades Lane, Dane in Shaw, Congleton, Cheshire CW12 3LL; tel: 01260 279276, fax: 01260 298913.

Visual Publications: The Green, Northleach, Cheltenham GL54 3EX; tel: 01451 860519, fax: 01451 960215.

H.A.B. White: Priory Farm, Balscote, Banbury, Oxon OX15 6JL; tel: 01295 730629.

Nicholas Wood: 20 South Hill Park Gardens, Hampstead, London NW3 2TG; tel: 0171 794 4316.